The Catty Cookbook

Culinary Catnip for People!

Holly D. Webber
With Sandy Spots

CEDAR HILL PUBLISHING

The Catty Cookbook ~ Culinary Catnip for People!

"There is no need for a piece of sculpture in a home that has a cat."
~ Wesley Bates

Front cover design and illustrations by Amanda Penrose, http://amanda.dd.com.au

Book design & back cover design by Rebecca Hayes

Photographs by Holly D. Webber, Foothill Felines Bengals and Savannahs

Published in the United States by
Cedar Hill Publishing
P.O. Box 905
Snowflake, Arizona 85937
http://www.cedarhillpublishing.com

Library of Congress Control Number 2005921229

ISBN 1-933324-01-5

This book is dedicated to my mother,
Sallie Rankin Davison,
whom I love and cherish with all my heart. Her support and encouragement
have been the strongest influences in my life. No words can ever express the
gratitude I have for the countless gifts she has given to me over the years,
including the most precious gift of all – that of being my mother. She is a
woman of unsurpassed compassion, rock-steady wisdom, ingenious creativity,
unique beauty, both inside and outside, and unending love.

Acknowledgments

Sincere appreciation and gratitude are extended to Becky Hayes, Amanda Penrose, Sallie Davison, Dorothy Davison, Wesley Webber, Kristin Johnson, Beth Bearry, Lori Simes, Linda Bosnich, Chuck and Barb Marsh, Wanda McDonald, Dale and Holly Hummel, Phil Mireles, the caring staff at Reagor Pet Hospital, Carmichael, CA, Bobbie, Scott and all the crew at Western Feed & Pet Supply, Carmichael, CA, the great folks and ambience of Cafe Milan in Playa del Rey, CA, Steffi Blitzstein, Ed Kerr and all the members of the HDW Chat Board for Cat Lovers - for their creative ideas, valued contributions, and belief in this book.

Special thanks go to my Bengal and Savannah cats for being their sweet selves in front of my camera: Sunny Spots, Sandy Spots, Vida Mia, Manzanita, MaiTai, Mochamelo, Malamute, Michabo, and Major Mews... as well as all the fabulous Foothill Felines kittens.

Sandy's Catty House Rules

"For me, one of the pleasures of cats' company is their devotion to bodily comfort."
- Sir Compton Mackenzie

1. The cat is not allowed in the house.
2. O.K. the cat is allowed in the house but not on the furniture.
3. Never mind ... the cat is allowed on the old furniture only.
4. Fine. The cat can be on all the furniture, but is definitely not allowed in the kitchen.
5. The cat is allowed in the kitchen, but can't jump up on the counters.
6. Okay, then, the cat can be on the counters, but must not sample the recipes.
7. The cat can eat the whole dish as long as there are some crumbs left for the rest of us. However, the cat must not be allowed with the humans on the bed.
8. The cat can sleep on the bed but must not sleep under the covers or on the pillows.
9. Just kidding, the cat can sleep under the covers, but be on the pillows by invitation only.
10. Well... the cat can sleep under the covers and on the pillows every night.
11. Humans must ask permission to sleep under the covers with the cat. Only the cat can sleep on the pillows.
12. If the cat wants to dine on some "Catty Cookbook" gourmet cooking in bed, you might as well indulge him. Besides, he'll probably devour it anyway (and chew on the book, too).

Table of Contents

Wildly Wonderful Soups
Cat-isfaction guaranteed! 25

Meewowy Breads & Cereals
Kitties like to knead their dough! 33

Purry Good Vegetables
Our pick of the litter! 43

Cat's Pajamas Entrees
Absolutely no cat-napping allowed! 51

Magnificat Desserts
The purr-fect finale! 63

 **denotes Sandy's Catty Classic Recipes**

Howling Good Beverages (With Alcohol)

Guaranteed to PICKLE your whiskers!

"Catnip is vodka and whiskey to most cats."
- Carl Van Vechten

CATTY CAFE AMORE

Pour hot coffee into preheated tall mug. Add 1 oz. Amaretto and 1 oz. Cognac. Top with whipped cream sprinkled with cinnamon. Serve with straw and spoon. Serves 1.

CATTY CAFE CAPPUCCINO

7 1/2 oz. Dark Crème de Cacao
5 oz. Amaretto
2 1/2 oz. White rum
1 1/2 oz. White Crème de Menthe
1/4 teaspoon vanilla extract
Fresh hot coffee
Whipped cream and shaved chocolate (garnish)

Combine all liqueurs in pitcher. Divide among preheated mugs and fill each with coffee to within 1/2" of rim. Add dollop of whipped cream to each and top with chocolate. Serve with a straw and spoon. Serves 8.

CATTY CAFE COCOA

1 Tablespoon unsweetened cocoa
1 Tablespoon granulated sugar
1 Tablespoon water
dash of salt
1 cup hot Half and Half
1 cup hot coffee
3 oz. (1/4 cup plus 2 Tablespoons) Almond Liqueur

Combine cocoa, sugar, water and salt in small saucepan and heat just to boiling. Stir in hot Half and Half, coffee and liqueur. Serve in heated mugs. Serves 2.

CATTY CAFE COFFEE

6 oz. Hot, strong coffee or espresso
1 oz. (2 Tablespoons) cream
2 teaspoons sugar
2 oz. (1/4 cup) Kahlua
1/4 teaspoon vanilla extract

Whipped cream flavored with instant coffee

Combine coffee, cream, sugar, liqueur and vanilla together in a heated mug. Top with a dollop of whipped cream, and serve with straw and spoon. Serves 1.

CATTY CAFE FLAMING LEMON

24 oz. Hot coffee
3 Tablespoons fresh lemon juice
2 jiggers (1/4 cup plus 2 Tablespoons) Anisette
4 thin lemon slices
dash nutmeg

Combine coffee and lemon juice in hot chafing dish. Heat anisette gently in separate small pan or pot, ignite, and immediately pour into chafing dish, stirring constantly until flame dies. Serve immediately in heated cups with lemon slice sprinkled with nutmeg floating on top. Makes 4 servings.

FROZEN DAIQUIRI

1/2 oz. Triple Sec
1 1/2 oz. Light rum
1 oz. Lemon/Lime juice

Combine ingredients in blender with 2 ice cubes until smooth. Serve in an on-the-rocks glass. Serves 1.

GOLDEN CADILLACS

2 oz. Galliano
4 oz. White Crème de Cacao
4 oz. Half & Half cream
tiny pinch of nutmeg

Place with small amount of ice in a blender and mix on low speed briefly. Sprinkle with nutmeg. Serves 2.

HOLIDAY CHAMPAGNE COCKTAIL

1/2 glass champagne
1/2 glass cranberry cocktail

Serve cold, without ice.

HOMEMADE KAHLUA

2 cups brandy
3 cups granulated sugar
3/4 cup instant coffee
2 cups boiling water
1 whole vanilla bean

Mix coffee and sugar in large bowl. Pour boiling water over and stir until dissolved. Add brandy. Pour into sterile bottles and/or containers. Cut vanilla bean into 3/4" pieces and add to Kahlua in each container. Seal tightly and label - let age for at least 30 days before using.

HOT EGGNOG

3 cups whole milk
1/2 cup whipping cream
4 egg yolks, well beaten
3/4 cup powdered sugar
1/4 teaspoon ground nutmeg
1 to 2 cups bourbon
4 egg whites, beaten until stiff

Heat milk and cream in top of double boiler over hot but not boiling water. Place egg yolks, sugar and nutmeg in a mixing bowl and mix well. Add hot milk mixture to egg yolk mixture gradually, stirring constantly. Return mixture to double boiler. Heat 5 minutes, stirring constantly. Pour mixture into warmed serving bowl and slowly stir in bourbon. Fold in egg whites. Serves 12.

HOT SPICED HOLIDAY PUNCH

1 cup water
1/2 cup granulated sugar
2 sticks cinnamon
1 teaspoon whole cloves
1 teaspoon whole allspice
1 - 18 oz. Can pineapple juice
1 - 18 oz. Can grapefruit juice
1 - 12 oz. Can apricot nectar
1/2 cup lemon juice
2 cups rose wine (optional)
Orange slices
Additional whole cloves

Combine water and sugar in a medium saucepan. Add cinnamon, cloves and allspice. Bring to a boil and boil 3 minutes. Strain out spices. Return syrup to saucepan and add pineapple and grapefruit juices, apricot nectar, lemon juice and wine (if desired). Heat until hot but do not boil. Serve hot in mugs or punch cups garnished with orange slices studded with whole cloves. Makes 2 to 2 1/2 quarts.

NOT SO REGULAR MARGARITA

1 - 6 oz. Container frozen limeade
1 can 7-Up®
1 can tequila

Mix in blender with ice cubes. Serve cold.

PARTY TIME MARGARITAS
(Serves 12)

6 limes, cut into wedges
Margarita salt
1 - 12 oz. Can frozen limeade
3 oz. Triple Sec
8 oz. Tequila
Ice cubes

Rub margarita glass rims with lime wedge, then dip in salt. Mix limeade, Triple Sec and tequila in blender -- add ice cubes and blend to a slushy consistency. Pour carefully into glasses; garnish with lime wedges if desired.

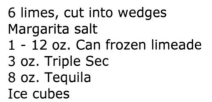

SINGAPORE SLING

1 oz. Sloe Gin
1/2 oz. Cherry Flavored Brandy
1 oz. gin
1 oz. Lemon juice

Combine in blender with 4 ice cubes. Pour unstrained into chilled tall glass. Top with soda; garnish with orange slice. Serves 1.

SNUGGLER

Add 1 1/2 oz. Peppermint Schnapps to a mug of hot chocolate. Top with whipped cream and snuggle up next to your favorite kitty. Yummy!

Sandy Spots

"Cats are living adornments."
- Edwin Lent

Howling Good Beverages
(No Alcohol)
Guaranteed to TICKLE your whiskers!

"A little lion, small and dainty sweet,
with sea-green eyes and softly stepping feet."
- Graham Tomson

BLACKBERRY TWIST

2 cups frozen blackberries, with juice
1 cup lemonade, made from concentrate
1 cup club soda
1/2 cup granulated sugar
1 quart ginger ale
8 lemon twists

Combine all ingredients except for ginger ale in a blender; blend until smooth (about 25 seconds). Put some ice cubes in tall chilled glasses or mugs, and add the blender mixture until containers are half filled. Fill remaining half of containers with ginger ale. Stir carefully, and top with a lemon twist. Serves 8.

CATTY PEANUT BUTTER COFFY

1 cup strong, cold, black coffee
1 cup whole milk
1 Tablespoon plus 1 teaspoon creamy peanut butter
2 Tablespoons granulated sugar

Place all ingredients into a blender and blend at least 2 minutes, until very smooth. Serve over ice in tall glasses. Makes 2 large servings.

DELIGHT-FUR SPRING SMOOTHIE

1 quart light cream
1 cup apricot nectar
1 - 20 oz. Can crushed pineapple
1/3 cup granulated sugar
1 teaspoon Grenadine syrup
fresh or canned pineapple cubes for garnish

Combine all ingredients except garnish in a blender and blend well until very smooth. Pour into chilled glasses and add the garnish of pineapple cubes. Makes 6 tall servings.

FRUIT CHILLER

1 quart orange juice
1 cup pineapple juice
1 cup grapefruit juice
1 pint raspberry sherbet

Make sure all the juices are chilled well. Mix chilled juices into a large pitcher. Pour over cracked ice in tall glasses and add a scoop of raspberry sherbet to each glass. Serve each glass with a straw and a long handled spoon.

HOMEMADE CRANBERRY JUICE

1 pound fresh, washed and stemmed cranberries
2 cups granulated sugar
6 cups water

Place all ingredients together in a 2-quart saucepan and bring to a full boil. Reduce heat and simmer until the cranberries burst open and are softened. Place a sieve over a large mixing bowl and line it with cheesecloth. Strain the cranberry juice through the cheesecloth. Chill cranberry juice in glass pitcher in the refrigerator. When ready to serve, pour over ice into tall glasses.

HOT CHOCOLATE DELIGHT

1 ounce unsweetened baking chocolate
1/4 cup granulated sugar
1/2 teaspoon vanilla
1/2 teaspoon ground cinnamon
pinch of salt
3 cups milk
whipped cream or large marshmallows

Melt chocolate in top of double boiler, being careful not to burn it. Add the milk and seasonings, and stir well. Continue to cook over the heat, stirring constantly, until very hot but not boiling. Serve in coffee mugs with either whipped cream or marshmallows on top.

ICED CATTY COFFY

2 cups hot, strong black coffee or half
coffee/half espresso
1/2 teaspoon bitters
1/2 teaspoon vanilla
1 Tablespoon granulated sugar
12 coffee flavored ice cubes (see below)
1 quart club soda

Add the coffee, bitters, vanilla and sugar to a
large pitcher (not glass - be sure to use a
container or pitcher that is resistant to heat).
Stir ingredients well set aside to let cool.
When cool, get out 6 tall glasses and place 2
coffee ice cubes in each glass. Divide the
cooled coffee mixture equally among the
glasses and fill to the top with club soda.
Delicious!

Coffee Flavored Ice Cubes:
Carefully pour cooled strong black coffee into
ice cube trays, being careful not to overfill.
Freeze well. To un-mold, first dip ice tray in
hot water.

MINT LEMONADE

4 large lemons
1/4 cup sugar
24 fresh mint leaves, washed
Lemon slices and/or mint leaves for garnish

Squeeze the lemons to make 1 cup of liquid,
and pour the juice into a quart jar. Add the
sugar and fill the jar with 3 cups of filtered,
cold water. Cover tightly and shake until the
sugar dissolves. Taste and add more lemon
or sugar as needed.

To serve, pour 1 cup into a blender. Add 6
mint leaves and a handful of ice, and process
until slushy. Pour into a glass, garnish with a
lemon slice or mint leaf and serve
immediately with a tall straw. Repeat with
the remaining ingredients. Serves 4.

PINK PUDDYTAT

1 teaspoon grenadine
1 teaspoon sugar
1 teaspoon fresh lime juice
1/2 cup bitter lemon
1/2 cup pink grapefruit juice

Mix grenadine, sugar and lime juice together
in a small pitcher. Add bitter lemon and
grapefruit juice and stir well. Puddy likes her
drink in a large brandy snifter! Place some
ice cubes in the bottom of Puddy's snifter,
then pour drink mixture over top and stir.
Serves 1 puddytat.

STRAWBERRY WATER

1 pint ripe strawberries, washed and
stemmed
2 quarts water
2 cups granulated sugar
Additional whole strawberries, washed and
unstemmed, for garnish

Crush strawberries slightly by putting them in
a large mixing bowl and pushing against them
with the back of a wooden spoon. Add just
enough to cover them, and let stand for 1
hour.

Strain the strawberries, reserving the liquid.
Wrap the strained strawberries in several
layers of cheesecloth and squeeze over the
bowl of strained liquid. Now add the 2 quarts
of water and the 2 cups of sugar. Stir
together well, and then strain again into a
glass pitcher that can be kept in the
refrigerator. When ready to serve, pour well
chilled strawberry water into medium glasses.

SUN TEA

3 quarts cold water
8 tea bags
sugar and lemon to taste
fresh mint sprigs for garnish

In the morning, place the tea bags in the cold water inside a large glass pot. Set the pot outside in a sunny spot (where it will stay sunny all day; otherwise, you will need to move the pot with the sun). At dinner time, remove the tea bags and add sugar and lemon to taste. Serve over ice in tall glasses, garnished with a mint sprig in each glass.

WATERMELONADE

1 medium, ripe watermelon (yield = 6 cups juice)
2 cups orange juice
1 cup lemon juice
2 cups granulated sugar, dissolved in 2 cups hot water
1 - 18 oz. Bottles 7-Up®

Cut the watermelon in half by using a scalloping technique. (Use a very sharp knife and make 1 1/2" cuts in a zigzag pattern around the center of the watermelon as it lays on its side, from one end to the other end. Cut as deeply with the knife held perpendicular to the watermelon as you can. You can make one large bowl by cutting closer to the top of the watermelon, or, for 2 bowls and if you are feeling especially frisky about your technique, try to cut the melon in two equal halves.) Carefully pull two halves apart, and select which one to use for your bowl.

Remove the seeds from both halves of the watermelon, and puree the pulp in a blender. (This should yield about 6 cups of juice.) Combine the watermelon juice, the orange and lemon juices, and the dissolved sugar in water into a large glass pitcher, and stir well. When ready to serve, place some whole ice cubes in the melon bowl and then carefully pour the juice mixture. Lastly, mix in the 7-Up®. May want to add thinly sliced oranges for garnish before ladling into punch cups.

Pitter-Patter Appetizers

Tiny pawprints of happiness!

"The smallest feline is a masterpiece."
- Leonardo da Vinci

APPETIZER MINI-QUICHES

Baked in muffin pans, each quiche appetizer is about 2 bites!! You can easily vary the fillings, and they are great made a day ahead. They reheat well and can be served warm or at room temperature.

Prepare enough pastry for a double crust 9" pie using a pie crust mix or your favorite recipe (or, gently thaw out frozen pie crusts), adding the following seasoning to the dry ingredients depending upon the filling you choose: Add 1/4 Teaspoon dill weed for the "Shrimp & Olive"; 1/2 Teaspoon caraway seed for the "Bacon & Mushroom"; 1/2 Teaspoon chile powder for the "Ham & Green Chile", or 2 Teaspoons parsley flakes for the "Clam & Bacon" filled quiches.

On a lightly floured board, roll out the dough 1/16" thick. Cut out 42 circles, using a 3" cutter (or the inside of a glass); re-roll scraps of dough as needed. Fit circles into bottoms and slightly up the sides of lightly greased 2 1/2" muffin pans. Divide filling equally among muffin cups. Lightly beat together 5 eggs, then add 1 2/3 Cups sour cream and stir until smooth. Spoon about 1 Tablespoon over filling into each muffin cup. Bake in a 375 degree oven until puffed and light brown, about 20-25 minutes. Cool in the pan 5 minutes before lifting out. Serve warm or let cool on wire racks. If made ahead, wrap cooled quiches airtight and refrigerate overnight. Reheat, uncovered, in a 350 degree oven for about 10 minutes. Makes 3 1/2 dozen appetizers.

SHRIMP & OLIVE FILLING:

In a bowl, mix together 1/3 pound small cooked shrimp, coarsely chopped; 1 can (2 1/2 oz.) sliced ripe black olives, drained; 1/3 Cup chopped green onions; and 1 2/3 Cups (about 7 oz.) shredded Swiss cheese. Divide this filling among muffin cups. Add a pinch cayenne to egg and sour cream mixture, then spoon about 1 Tablespoon into each cup.

BACON & MUSHROOM FILLING:

Fry 8 slices thick bacon until crisp, then drain and crumble. Chop 1/4 pound fresh mushrooms and sauté them in 1 Tablespoon butter or margarine until limp and the mushroom liquid evaporates. Combine bacon, mushrooms, 1/3 Cup chopped green onion and 1 2/3 Cups shredded Swiss or jack cheese. Divide among muffin cups; add egg mixture.

HAM & GREEN CHILE FILLING:

In a bowl, mix together 3/4 to 1 Cup finely diced cooked ham (about 3 oz.), 3-4 Tablespoons chopped canned California green chiles, 1/4 Cup chopped green onion, and 1 2/3 Cups shredded jack cheese. Divide among muffin cups; add egg mixture.

CLAM & BACON FILLING:

Fry 3 slices thick bacon until crisp, then drain and crumble. Combine bacon with 2 cans (6 1/2 oz. Each) chopped clams, well drained; 1/3 Cup chopped green onion; and 1 2/3 Cups shredded Swiss cheese. Divide among muffin cups. Add a pinch of garlic powder to the egg mixture, then spoon into cups.

BAGEL CHIPS

6 day-old bagels (preferably onion, sesame, rye, or other savory flavors)
1 Tbsp. Extra virgin olive oil
1 Tbsp. Onion powder
1 Tbsp. Garlic salt (can substitute garlic powder)
1 Tbsp. Seasoned salt

Heat oven to 200 degrees. Line several baking sheets with aluminum foil. Slice the bagels crosswise into 1/4 inch thick rounds or planks. Arrange in a single layer on the baking sheets. Using a spray mister, lightly coat the tops with the olive oil, then generously sprinkle the chips with equal amounts of the onion powder, garlic salt and seasoned salt. Bake until crisp and cracker-like, 45 minutes. Store in a tightly covered container for up to a week. Serve as appetizers with all kinds of dips and spreads.

CANAPES

10 oz. Gouda cheese, softened
2 Tablespoons butter
1 cup crumbled Roquefort cheese
1 cup grated Cheddar cheese
dash Tabasco® sauce
1 teaspoon Worcestershire® sauce
1 teaspoon prepared mustard
3 Tablespoons half and half (light cream)
3 Tablespoons sherry

Mix well; serve with crackers.

CHEESE PUFFS

1 glass Old English Kraft® cheese
1 cup all-purpose flour
1/4 cup oleo (shortening)
1/2 teaspoon Tabasco® sauce
1/4 teaspoon salt

Combine all ingredients together in a bowl and form into small balls with clean hands. Bake at 425 degrees for 12 minutes. Serve hot. Refrigerate or freeze leftovers.

CHEESE TEMPTERS

3 oz. Sharp shredded Cheddar cheese (room temperature)
1/4 cup butter or margarine (room temperature)
1/2 cup sifted all-purpose flour
1/4 teaspoon salt
1 cup Corn Flakes
Paprika

Combine cheese and butter until well blended. Add flour and salt; mix well. Add corn flakes to mixture and blend with clean hands until it "holds together". Pinch off small amounts, roll into 3/4" balls. Place on ungreased baking sheet 2" apart. Sprinkle with paprika and bake for 12 minutes at 400 degrees. Makes 28-30 tempter balls.

CREAMY CAMEMBERT SPREAD

3 portions (1 1/2 oz. Each) Camembert cheese
1 - 8 oz. Package cream cheese
2 cups (2 - 8 oz. Containers or 1 - 16 oz. Container) creamed cottage cheese
1/2 cup each grated Parmesan and Romano cheese
1/2 teaspoon seasoned salt

Let Camembert and cream cheeses soften in medium-sized mixing bowl at room temperature. Beat together until smooth. Add cottage cheese, grated cheeses and seasoned salt. Combine and turn into serving bowl. Makes 3 1/2 cups. Delicious on assorted crackers or salty rye bread.

CREOLE PEANUT ROLL

1 pound Roquefort cheese (room temperature)
1/2 pound cream cheese (room temperature)
1 medium yellow onion, grated
2 Tablespoons cognac
dash of Tabasco® sauce
chopped peanuts

Combine cheeses with onion, cognac and Tabasco®. Mix very thoroughly and form into a long roll, 1 1/2" in diameter. Chill overnight in refrigerator. The next day, roll in enough chopped peanuts to completely cover the cheese. Slice and serve on round crackers. Serves 12.

DELICIOUS CAKE SPREAD

2 - 4 1/2 oz. Cans deviled ham
1 teaspoon instant minced onion
1 - 8 oz. Package cream cheese
1/4 cup sour cream
finely chopped nuts
freshly chopped parsley and other green herbs

Mix ham and onion and form into a 5 to 6" square on a serving plate. Blend cheese and sour cream together and use to "frost" the "cake" (ham). Pat nuts and herbs on the sides and top of cake. Chill in refrigerator. Serve as a dip for crackers. Very pretty!

DILLY DIP

1 small carton sour cream, and an
   equal amount of Best Foods® mayonnaise
1 Tablespoon dill weed
1 teaspoon Beau Monde
1 Tablespoon minced or fresh onion
1 teaspoon minced or fresh parsley

Mix all ingredients well and let stand in refrigerator an hour to bring out flavor. Serve chilled with assorted crackers and chips.

ELEGANT DIP FOR CRACKERS & SMALL TOASTS

8 oz. Softened cream cheese
2 Tablespoons sour cream
1 Tablespoon lemon or lime juice
1/4 teaspoon Worcestershire® sauce
1 teaspoon curry powder
1/2 yellow onion, shredded for the juice
Beaumonde seasoning, to taste

Mix above ingredients together well, serve chilled with crackers or small pieces of toasted bread.

GIBBER'S CHRISTMAS CHEESE BALLS

(This is for mass production & gift giving!!)

MILD VERSION:

9 - 8 oz. Cream cheese packages
1 pkg. (4 Cups) walnut pieces
3 small cans chopped black olives
5 to 6 diced green onions
1 diced green pepper

Seasonings: Worcestershire® sauce, Tabasco® sauce, garlic powder

Mix everything together by hand but set aside 1 1/2 cups of the nuts. Form into about 13 individual appetizer balls and chill balls in refrigerator on wax paper until firm enough to hold their shape while rolling to coat them in remaining nuts. Wrap in saran and then foil, and tie with holiday green ribbon. Freeze until ready to use or to give as gifts.

HOTTER VERSION:

3 large Velveeta® packages
3 small Jalapeno Velveeta® packages
3/4 cup finely chopped yellow onion
3/4 cup finely chopped celery
1/2 cup finely chopped fresh parsley
4 cups chopped pecans

Mix everything together by hand, setting aside 1 1/2 cups of the pecans. Form into about 18 individual appetizer balls and chill balls in refrigerator on wax paper until firm enough to hold their shape while rolling to coat them in remaining nuts. Wrap in saran and then foil, and tie with holiday red ribbon to distinguish hotter cheese balls from the milder version. Freeze until ready to use or to give as gifts.

GOLD FINGERS

4 cups chicken broth
1/4 cup butter
1 cup polenta
2 cloves fresh garlic, minced
1 cup Mozzarella & Italian blend shredded cheese
1/3 cup finely chopped roasted red bell pepper
1/2 cup shredded Parmesan cheese
1/4 cup sliced green onions (green tops only)
1/2 Tablespoon minced fresh sage
salt and pepper to taste

Spray a 13 inch x 9 inch baking pan with non-stick cooking spray; set aside. In a medium saucepan, bring broth and butter to a boil. Add polenta; cook and stir over low heat for 10 minutes. Add remaining ingredients and cook for 5 minutes more. Pour mixture into prepared pan and let cool to room temperature or chill overnight. Cut into 1-by-2 inch strips and transfer to a decorative platter. Serve at room temperature. Or, if desired, brush lightly with virgin olive oil and grill for several minutes on each side until lightly browned. Makes 24 strips; recipe can be doubled.

GUACAMOLE

2 medium ripe avocados, halved
juice of 1 lemon
1/2 cup finely chopped onion
1/2 cup chopped tomato
1/2 teaspoon salt
2 Tablespoons minced cilantro

Using a large spoon, scoop the avocado from the shells leaving about a 1/8" rim. Squeeze the lemon juice over the empty avocado shell halves and the pulp. Mash the avocado pulp and combine with the remaining ingredients to make the guacamole filling. Return the filling to the shells if desired, or serve in small serving bowl garnished with fresh cilantro sprig; serve the same day with tortilla chips.

HEAVENLY DIP

3 ripe avocados, mashed with dash of Worcestershire®, juice of 1/2 lemon, dash of onion salt and garlic salt.

Spread avocado mixture on a dinner plate. Then top with layers as follows: Chopped red tomatoes; chopped red onions; 1/2 cup shredded cheddar cheese; 1/2 cup shredded jack cheese; 1/2 cup sliced ripe black olives.

Keep refrigerated. Serve with triangular heavy corn chips for dipping.

HOMEMADE SALSA

1 - 1 lb. 14 oz. Can stewed tomatoes, chopped
2 fresh yellow chiles, chopped
2 fresh mild green chiles, chopped
2 fresh medium hot green chiles, chopped
1 fresh mild red chile, chopped
1 small to medium fresh yellow onion, chopped
Dash garlic salt
Dash chile pepper (season to taste)
Dash regular salt and pepper
1 Tablespoon extra virgin olive oil
3 Tablespoons fresh chopped cilantro

Combine above ingredients together. For hotter salsa, use seeds from the fresh chile peppers. For milder salsa, do not use seeds from chiles, and use more mild chiles and less hot chiles. Refrigerate. Serves 10 - 12. Ole!!

HOT CHILE CHEESE APPETIZERS

1/4 cup butter
10 eggs
1/2 cup all-purpose flour
1 teaspoon baking powder
dash of salt
2 - 4 oz. Cans chopped green chiles
1 pint cottage cheese
1 pound Jack cheese, shredded

In a 9" x 12" Pyrex flat pan, melt butter inside pan in the oven. Beat eggs slightly in a large bowl. Add flour, baking powder and salt to eggs, and blend well. Add melted butter, chiles, cottage cheese and Jack cheese and mix until blended. Turn into pan and bake at 400 degrees for 15 minutes; reduce heat to 350 degrees and bake another 35 to 40 minutes. Let set for 10 minutes before cutting into squares.

HOT CLAM DIP

2 pounds (4 - 8 oz. Packages) softened cream cheese
4 cans (6 1/2 oz. Each) minced clams (drain all but 1 can -- keep the juice from 1 can)
3 teaspoons Beau Monde seasoning
2 Tablespoons parsley flakes
1/2 teaspoon garlic
1 large round loaf of Shepherder bread

Cut the top off the bread and pull or cut out the insides (set aside and cut into pieces for dipping), leaving a nice, firm empty bread shell. Beat above ingredients together and fill the inside of the bread with clam mixture. Replace bread top and wrap completely in foil. Bake at 350 degrees for 2 hours. Serve warm with small pieces of Shepherder or French bread for dipping.

QUESADILLAS

1 medium ripe avocado
1 small can sliced black olives
6 each 6" flour tortillas
6 oz. Grated Mozzarella cheese
4 oz. Grated sharp Cheddar cheese
1/3 cup green bell pepper, seeded and diced
1/3 cup red bell pepper, seeded and diced
1/2 cup chopped tomato
1/2 cup fresh basil or cilantro, chopped

Cook tortillas in non-stick pan (or pan sprayed with Pam® non-stick olive oil coating) until crispy. Remove and top with equal portions of cheeses, peppers, tomato and fresh basil. Place tortillas on a cookie sheet in a preheated 300 degree oven for approximately 10 minutes or until cheese is melted and bubbly. Cut quesadillas into 6 pizza-style wedges and top each with a slice of avocado and some black olives.

SIMPLE SALSA DIP

Simply ... wonderful!! Take an 8 oz. Package of cream cheese and set in a serving bowl. Pour fresh medium hot salsa over top. Serve with corn tortilla chips of different colors, if available. The longer this dip sits out and is enjoyed, the better it gets as the flavors mingle!

Another FUR-bulous version: Take an 8 oz. Package of cream cheese and set in a serving bowl. Pour contents of a jar of Jalapeno Mint jelly over the top, and serve as above!

SMOKY SALMON SPREAD

2 - 3 oz. Packages sliced smoked salmon
1 - 8 oz. Package cream cheese, softened
2 Tablespoons whipping cream
2 Tablespoons lemon juice
garlic salt
Assorted crackers, chips, pretzels or small bagels

Dice or chop sliced smoked salmon. Combine with cream cheese, cream, lemon juice and garlic salt to taste. Mix well and spread into 1 1/2 cup mold or shape as desired. Chill thoroughly. Unmold onto platter and place crackers, chips, pretzels and small bagels around the outside of the spread. Garnish with lemon slices and sliced salmon strips if desired. Makes about 1 1/2 cups.

SPINACH DIP

1 package frozen chopped spinach, thawed and drained well
1 small jar marinated artichoke hearts, drained
1/2 cup chopped fresh parsley
1/2 cup chopped green onions
1/2 teaspoon salt
1/2 teaspoon freshly ground pepper
1 cup mayonnaise

Chop the marinated artichoke hearts into small pieces. Combine all ingredients and let stand 2-3 hours or longer. Serve with crackers.

SWEET & SOUR MEATBALL APPETIZERS

2 1/2 pounds lean ground beef
1/2 cups bread crumbs
1 teaspoon salt
Dash of pepper
2 - 8 oz. Cans tomato sauce
1 cup water
1 - 8 oz. Can sauerkraut, undrained
1/2 cup brown sugar, firmly packed
1 cup golden raisins
1 medium onion, chopped

Combine beef, crumbs, salt and pepper. Mix thoroughly but lightly. Shape into 3/4" balls. Combine tomato sauce, water, sauerkraut, brown sugar, raisins and onion in a medium saucepan. Bring to boil, then drop in meatballs. Cover and simmer for 1 1/2 hours. Serve with toothpicks. Makes about 8-10 servings.

TALL TAIL ROLL-UPS

10 Tablespoons butter, divided
4 cups coarsely chopped mushrooms (portabella, shiitake, white or brown, or any combination)
3 cloves fresh garlic, minced
1 cup shredded Gruyere cheese
1 Tablespoon chopped fresh sage
1 Tablespoon chopped fresh marjoram
1/4 teaspoon salt
1/4 teaspoon freshly ground black pepper
1 - 16-oz. Box frozen phyllo dough, thawed

Preheat oven to 400 degrees. Melt 2 Tablespoons butter in a large skillet. Add mushrooms and garlic; cook for 10 minutes, stirring frequently. Remove from heat and let cool slightly, then stir in cheese and seasonings. Melt remaining 8 Tablespoons butter in a small bowl. Unroll phyllo dough. Place 1 sheet dough on a cutting board and cover remaining sheets with a damp cloth. Brush very lightly with butter. Spread a thin line of about 1 Tablespoon mushroom filling along one edge of the phyllo sheet and roll up tightly to enclose; twist ends and place on a parchment-lined baking sheet. Repeat with remaining phyllo dough sheets and filling. Bake for 10 minutes or until golden brown and crisp. Serve warm. Makes about 15 roll-ups; recipe may be doubled.

Catty Notes

Paws-itively Scrumptious Salads

Dressing up the catnip!

"God made the cat in order that man might have the pleasure of caressing the tiger."
- Fernand Mery

AVOCADO MUSHROOM SALAD

1/3 cup extra virgin olive oil
1 Tablespoon dry white wine
2 Tablespoons fresh chopped parsley
1 clove garlic, crushed
1 teaspoon salt
freshly ground black pepper
juice of 1 lemon
2 avocados, thinly sliced in rings
1/2 pound mushrooms, thinly sliced
parsley for garnish

Combine oil, wine, chopped parsley, garlic, salt, pepper and lemon juice. Layer sliced avocados and mushrooms on serving platter. Carefully pour dressing over and marinate 1 hour. Garnish with parsley sprigs.

Serves 4-6.

B.J.'s OLD FASHIONED COLESLAW

Cook 1/2 pound bacon until crisp; reserve drippings and crumble the bacon.
Slice 1 medium cabbage in thin shreds.

Mix and pour over cabbage:
1/4 cup bacon fat
1/4 cup vinegar
1/2 cup mayonnaise
1 Tablespoon granulated sugar
1/2 teaspoon dry mustard
1 teaspoon salt
1/2 teaspoon freshly ground pepper
2 Tablespoons grated onion
1/2 cup finely grated celery
crumbled bacon

BEAN SPROUT SALAD

Lettuce (use two different kinds -- select for differences in color and texture), torn into bite-sized pieces
1 package fresh bean sprouts
1 can de-veined shrimp
Handful of sliced almonds, lightly browned in butter in a saucepan

Add bean sprouts, shrimp and sliced almonds to lettuce. Just before serving, add dressing (see below) to salad mixture and toss lightly.

DRESSING:
Thin mayonnaise with a little milk, and add 1 teaspoon soy sauce and 1/2 teaspoon curry powder. More soy sauce and curry powder can be added to taste.

BENGAL SALAD

1 cup cooked crab
1 cup cooked shrimp
1 - #2 can pineapple tidbits, drained, patted dry with paper towels
1/2 cup pine nuts
1/2 cup water chestnuts
1/4 cup chopped green onions
1 cup chopped celery
2 Tablespoons white raisins
Juice of 1 lemon
All these ingredients can be mixed ahead of time except the pine nuts.

Mix well, and serve with Bengal Dressing (see below)

BENGAL DRESSING:
1 cup mayonnaise
1/4 cup sour cream
1/2 teaspoon curry

Mix together, chill, and serve as topping for Bengal Salad. Serves 4.

BILTMORE SALAD

2 packages lime jello
2 cups hot water
3/4 cup fruit juice (orange or pineapple)
Combine above per jello package instructions and let set

1 cup whipped cream
2 Tablespoons mayonnaise
Beat jello with the cream and mayonnaise until mixture is a pale green color.

Add: 3/4 cup crushed pineapple (frozen or canned)
2 Tablespoons chopped green pepper
3/4 cup shredded cabbage
12 large marshmallows, quartered

Mix together and chill. Serves 16.

CATTY FRESH FRUIT SALAD CLASSIC

1 cup cantaloupe balls
1 cup Crenshaw melon balls
1 cup honeydew melon balls
1 cup watermelon balls, black seeds removed
1 cup sliced strawberries
1 cup washed seedless red grapes
1/3 cup orange juice, no pulp

Combine all ingredients in large bowl. Cover and refrigerate; serve cold in chilled bowls, garnished with mint leaves if desired. Makes 6 servings.

CHICKEN SALAD WITH GRAPES

4 cups boneless, skinned, cooked chicken breasts, cut up into small pieces
1 1/2 cups chopped celery
1 1/2 cups seedless grapes (red or green), halved
1 1/2 cups toasted almonds (optional)
4 chopped green onions
2 Tablespoons curry powder
salt and pepper to taste
1 1/2 cups lowfat yogurt (plain)
2/3 cup mayonnaise

Combine and adjust seasonings to taste. If too dry, add more yogurt to moisten. Serve chilled over large lettuce leaf. Serves 6.

FENNEL, MUSHROOM & PARMESAN SALAD

1 large bulb fennel (about 1 pound)
1 pound fresh, washed mushrooms
1/2 cup extra virgin olive oil

1/4 cup fresh squeezed lemon juice
1/4 cup minced green onions
4 sprigs fresh thyme, leaves only
3/4 teaspoon salt
1/4 teaspoon minced fresh garlic
freshly ground black pepper
1 ounce chunk Parmesan cheese

Trim the stalks and fronds from the fennel, reserving enough fronds to make 1/4 cup when chopped. Cut the bulb in quarters lengthwise and trim away the triangle of solid core at the base. Cut each quarter into thirds or quarters lengthwise and cut each of those in half crosswise.

Trim the tough bottoms of the mushroom stems and cut the mushrooms into quarter-inch slices.

In a large bowl, whisk together the olive oil, lemon juice, green onions, thyme leaves, the fennel fronds, salt and garlic, to mix ingredients well. Add the fennel and stir to coat. Remove the fennel with a slotted spoon, draining any excess dressing back into the bowl, and arrange the fennel on a platter in a broad, shallow layer.

Add the mushrooms to the leftover dressing, season to taste with black pepper and stir to coat well. Arrange the mushrooms in an oblong mound on top of the fennel, centering it so that the fennel is showing around the edges.

Using a vegetable peeler, shave large flakes of Parmesan cheese over the top of the salad. Serve immediately - makes 4-6 servings.

GOURMET SALAD

1/2 ripe avocado on a lettuce leaf, sprinkled with lemon juice, and cavity filled with canned, jellied red consommé and topped with sour cream and caviar. Serves 1.

GRUYERE SALAD

1 pound sharp Cheddar cheese, shredded
1 pound Gruyere cheese, shredded
1 cup sliced stuffed green olives (or may use black ripe olives)
2 bunches green onions, finely chopped

DRESSING:
1 cup extra virgin olive oil
1/4 cup wine vinegar
1 Tablespoon Dijon mustard
1 teaspoon salt
freshly ground pepper

Combine shredded cheeses, onions and olives. Mix dressing ingredients in separate bowl thoroughly and just before serving, toss lightly with cheese mixture.

HAWAIIAN SALAD

4 cups bean sprouts
1/2 cup diced red onion
1/2 cup diced green pepper
1 medium tomato, sliced
1 cup thinly sliced, peeled carrot
1/2 cup sliced celery
1/4 cup sliced water chestnuts or almonds
shredded or torn lettuce, any variety and amount desired
1 - 7 oz. Can tuna, drained
Dressing (see below)

Combine in bowl bean sprouts, red onion, green pepper, tomato, carrot, celery, water chestnuts, lettuce and tuna. Toss with Dressing or prepare salad and Dressing separately and chill well before serving. Serves 4 to 6.

DRESSING:
1/4 cup mayonnaise
1/4 cup Bleu cheese dressing
1/2 teaspoon curry powder
1/2 teaspoon ginger
salt and pepper

Combine all ingredients, adding salt and pepper to taste. Mix well, then serve over Hawaiian Salad.

HOLLY'S SPINACH SALAD

2 bunches fresh spinach
4 to 5 green onions
1 -2 whole sections string cheese
6 pieces of bacon, cooked
mayonnaise
white distilled vinegar

Wash spinach well, pat dry, and remove stems. Tear into bite-sized pieces. (May be stored in plastic bag at this point and refrigerated for use the following day.) Put spinach in a large mixing bowl. Add just enough mayonnaise to moisten. Slice and add green onions, including the tops; pull off and add fairly thin strings of the cheese; crumble and add the bacon. Sprinkle with vinegar to taste (should add just the right amount of "tartness") and mix well. Cover and refrigerate until ready to serve.

LAYERED BUFFET SALAD

1 large bunch fresh spinach
1 head red leaf lettuce
1 head butter lettuce
1 double package herb-flavored salad dressing mix (made with buttermilk and mayonnaise, like Hidden Valley Ranch® brand)
2 cups mayonnaise
1 cup dairy sour cream
1 cup plain yogurt
1 - 10 oz. Package frozen small peas, thawed
1 bunch green onions, chopped
4 hard-boiled eggs, sieved
1/4 pound bacon, cooked, drained and crumbled

Wash spinach, lettuces and pat dry. Break into small pieces. Combine salad dressing mix with mayonnaise, sour cream and yogurt. In a 13" x 9" baking dish, layer the following: spinach, red leaf lettuce, butter lettuce, peas, green onions, eggs, and crumbled bacon. Spread prepared dressing over top, being sure to seal all edges. Place in refrigerator overnight. Cut into squares to serve. Makes 12 servings.

MARGARET'S SALAD

Cup up iceberg lettuce into 1" squares, and place evenly on bottom of serving bowl. Spread lightly with mayonnaise to moisten. Place a layer of sliced sweet onion over the mayonnaise. Sprinkle with 1 Tablespoon sugar, 2 Tablespoons vinegar, 1/2 cup cooked baby green peas, 2 Tablespoons fresh lemon juice, 1 1/2 slices Swiss cheese cut into thin strips, and crumbled bacon. Make 2 hours ahead of time and serve well chilled.

POTATO SALAD

6 potatoes, boiled
3 eggs, hard boiled
1/2 to 3/4 cup mayonnaise
1/2 teaspoon salt
1/4 teaspoon pepper
1/2 to 1 teaspoon wine vinegar
1-2 Tablespoons chopped onion, optional

Mix all ingredients well in large bowl. Keep refrigerated; serve cold.

RASPBERRY SALAD

1 package raspberry jello
1 package frozen raspberries
3/4 cup hot water
1 can crushed pineapple

Prepare jello per package directions. When softly set, gently fold in the frozen raspberries and crushed pineapple.

SENATE SALAD

1 cup bite-size pieces iceberg lettuce
1 cup bite-size pieces romaine or escarole
1/2 cup bite size pieces water cress
1 1/2 cups diced fresh lobster meat
1 cup diced celery
1/2 cup chopped green onions, including stems
2 medium tomatoes, cubed
1 medium ripe avocado, peeled and cubed

5 large stuffed olives, sliced
sections from 1/2 a grapefruit
Garlic salad-dressing mix (made up per package directions)

Place ingredients, except salad dressing, in a large salad bowl. Toss lightly. Garnish salad top with lobster claws if desired. Serve with Garlic salad dressing. Makes 4 entree portions.

SHRIMP, AVOCADO & SWEET ONION SALAD

1 large sweet onion (about 1/4 pound)
3 large avocados
2 1/2 Tablespoons fresh lemon juice
1/4 cup virgin olive oil
1 teaspoon salt
2 Tablespoons minced chives, plus more for garnish
1 pound shrimp, cooked and peeled

Cut the onion in quarters lengthwise, then cut each quarter into lengthwise halves or thirds. Cut each of these sections in half crosswise. Place the onion pieces in a bowl of cold water to soak for 15 minutes.

Cut the avocados in half, then remove the pits and with a spoon, scoop out the flesh in one piece. Cut avocados into pieces the same size as the onions.

In a large bowl, whisk together the lemon juice, olive oil, salt and chives. Drain the onions and pat them dry with paper towel. Add the onions to the dressing and stir to coat well. Remove the onions with a slotted spoon, draining any excess dressing back into the bowl. Arrange onions on a platter in a broad layer.

Place the avocados in the remaining dressing and stir to coat well. Remove them with a slotted spoon and arrange them in an oblong mount on top of the onions, with the onions showing around the edges.

Add the shrimp to the remaining dressing, adding a bit more lemon juice and salt to

21

taste. Arrange the shrimp on top of the avocados and garnish with more minced chives. Serve right away. Serves 4-6.

SPECIAL DELIVERY SALAD

SALAD:
2 heads Romaine lettuce
2 peeled ripe tomatoes

CONDIMENTS:
1/4 cup chopped green onion
1/2 cup freshly grated Romano cheese
1 pound cooked, drained and finely chopped bacon
1/2 cup croutons

DRESSING:
3 oz. Extra virgin olive oil
juice of 2 lemons
1/2 teaspoon freshly ground pepper
1/4 teaspoon chopped fresh mint leaves
1/4 teaspoon oregano
1 coddled egg

Pour about 2 Tablespoons extra virgin olive oil into a large bowl. Sprinkle with salt and rub bottom and sides of bowl firmly with large clove of garlic. Remove garlic and in the bottom of the bowl, first place the tomatoes, cut into eighths, then add the Romaine lettuce, sliced into 1 inch strips. (At this point, you may add other vegetables to salad, if desired.) Add the condiments (except for the croutons), and mix well.

DRESSING:
Pour rest of extra virgin olive oil, lemon juice and seasons into a mixing bowl. Add coddled egg and whip vigorously. When ready to serve, pour dressing over salad, and add the croutons at the very last. Serves 8.

SUMMER JELLO SALAD

1 pkg. Sugar-free lime jello (3 oz. Or 6 oz.)
Fresh cantaloupe and watermelon, scooped into 3/4" melon balls
Seedless green grapes

Prepare jello according to directions and refrigerate until near congealed consistency. Fold in melon balls and grapes, and refrigerate in oblong glass dish until ready to serve. This recipe can also be poured into a mold.

SWEET-SOUR SUMMER VEGGIE SALAD

3 small zucchini, thinly sliced
3 small yellow squash, thinly sliced
1 red bell pepper, thinly sliced
1/2 red onion, thinly sliced

DRESSING:
1/2 cup red wine vinegar
1/3 cup granulated sugar
1/4 cup extra virgin olive oil
1/2 teaspoon salt
1 clove garlic, minced and mashed

In wide mouth 1 quart jar with tight lid, combine the vegetables. In saucepan, mix dressing ingredients and bring to a boil, adding garlic last. Pour dressing over vegetables in jar. Tightly close jar and turn jar frequently for at least 3 hours (preferably overnight). Drain and serve chilled over cupped lettuce leaf. This is a very pretty and delicious salad!!

TIMI'S CORNED BEEF SALAD

1/2 cup cold water
1 packet Knox® unflavored gelatin
1 can Consommé
2 Tablespoons lemon juice
1/2 cup green bell pepper, diced
1/2 cup celery, diced
1 Tablespoon green onions, diced
8 stuffed olives, sliced
1 can corned beef, cut into small pieces

3 hard boiled eggs, cut up
1/2 cup mayonnaise

Add the gelatin to the cold water. Heat the can of Consommé, and add remaining ingredients to large saucepan, stirring well. Remove from heat and put in the refrigerator to set. Serve over large lettuce leaf.

Catty Notes

Wildly Wonderful Soups
CAT-isfaction guaranteed!

"Cats seem to go on the principle that it never does any harm to ask for what you want."
- Joseph Krutch

B.J.'s SUMMER SOUP

1 cucumber, partially peeled and seeded, cut
into 2" pieces
1/2 avocado
2 scallions
1 cup chicken stock
1 cup sour cream
2 Tablespoons lime juice
salt and pepper to taste

Blend ingredients together in blender until
smooth and creamy. Chill soup for at least 3
hours. Serve in chilled bowls with lime slices
on top for garnish.

BETTY'S LIMA BEAN SOUP

1 package (10 oz.) frozen lima beans, cooked
until tender and drained
2 Tablespoons butter
1/3 cup green onions
1 teaspoon curry powder
1/2 cup cream
4 sprigs fresh parsley
1/2 teaspoon tarragon
salt to taste
1 can Campbell's® chicken broth (1 1/2 cups)

Put lima beans in blender. Add butter, green
onions and curry powder; blend well. Add
cream, parsley, tarragon and salt. Heat
chicken broth gently in large sauce pan. Add
ingredients carefully from blender and heat
while stirring to blend ingredients. Serve hot
- make sure not to bring to boiling point.
Serves 4-6.

BLACK BEAN SOUP

1 pound dried black or turtle beans
1/4 cup (1/2 stick) butter
1 small yellow onion, chopped
2 fresh garlic cloves, minced
2 quarts water (can substitute 1 quart with
inexpensive cooking sherry if desired for more
flavor)
2 celery stalks, chopped
1 ham bone or hock

Herb bouquet (few sprigs parsley, 1 bay leaf,
pinch of thyme, or other fresh herbs
available)
Salt and freshly ground pepper
1/4 cup sherry (or more to taste)
Lemon slices or chopped hard-cooked egg
(garnish)

Presoak beans at least 1 hour using quick-
soaking method. Drain and transfer to soup
pot or Dutch oven. Melt butter in small skillet
over medium-high heat. Add onion and garlic
and sauté until golden. Add beans with
water, celery, ham bone, herb bouquet, salt
and pepper. Cover and bring to a boil.
Reduce heat and simmer about 3 hours, or
until beans are very tender.

Discard bone and herb bouquet. Transfer
beans with remaining liquid to food processor,
blender, sieve or food mill and puree. Return
to soup pot, adding more water if mixture
seems too thick. Return to boil. Add sherry,
taste and adjust seasoning. Serve hot,
garnished with lemon slices or hard-cooked
egg.

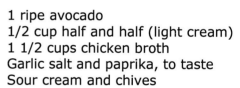

COLD AVOCADO SOUP

1 ripe avocado
1/2 cup half and half (light cream)
1 1/2 cups chicken broth
Garlic salt and paprika, to taste
Sour cream and chives

In blender, combine all but sour cream and
chives. Blend well, then chill the mixture.
When ready to serve, garnish with a dollop of
sour cream and a sprinkling of chives. Serves
2-3.

COLD FRENCH TARRAGON SOUP

Ladle into lettuce lined bowls for a refreshing
presentation before a summer luncheon.
Serves 4.

5 cups chicken stock
4 teaspoons chopped fresh tarragon or 2
Teaspoons dried and crumbled tarragon

1 envelope unflavored gelatin
1 cup cold water
1/4 pound cooked shrimp, coarsely chopped
Chopped fresh parsley
Fresh lemon juice
Lemon slices

Bring chicken stock to boil in saucepan. Reduce heat and simmer 5 minutes. Add tarragon. Dissolve gelatin in water and add to hot stock, mixing well. Remove from heat and let cool. Cover and chill for at least 4 hours. Stir soup gently and ladle into individual bowls. Sprinkle each serving with some shrimp, parsley and lemon juice, and top with a lemon slice.

COLD MELON SOUP

Serve slightly cooler than room temperature in crystal or glass stemware for added elegance before a summer brunch or festive dinner. Serves 6-8.

3 cups coarsely chopped cantaloupe
3 cups coarsely chopped honeydew melon
2 cups fresh orange juice
1/3 cup fresh lime juice
1 Tablespoon honey (more or less depending upon sweetness of melons)
2 cups Brut Champagne or dry white wine
Fresh mint leaves (garnish)

Finely chop half of cantaloupe and honeydew and set aside. Puree remaining melon in batches with orange and lime juices and honey in processor or blender. Pour into large bowl. Stir in Champagne or wine and reserved melon. Cover and chill several hours. Garnish each serving with mint leaves.

CREAM OF SPLIT PEA SOUP

1 pound dry split peas
water
1 quart chicken stock
1/4 pound salt pork, cut in about 12 pieces
2 medium yellow onions, chopped
3 leeks, coarsely chopped

3 medium potatoes, peeled and cut in chunks
salt and pepper
2 cups whipping cream
2 Tablespoons butter or margarine

Soak peas in enough cold water to cover. Bring to boil, cover and simmer 1 hour. Drain and place peas in heavy kettle with 1 quart water, chicken stock, salt pork, onions, leeks and potatoes.

Lightly season with salt and pepper, then bring to boil. Cover and simmer 1 1/2 to 2 hours or until peas are well-cooked. Remove pork bits and puree soup in food processor or blender. Return to pot, bring to boil and stir in cream. Heat gently 3 to 5 minutes. Stir in butter and serve. Makes about 12 servings.

CREAM OF VEGETABLE SOUP

3/4 cup (1 1/2 sticks) butter
3/4 cup diced onion
1 1/2 cups diced potatoes
3/4 cup peeled diced tomato
3/4 cup diced carrots
3/4 cup diced green beans
3/4 cup coarsely chopped broccoli
3/4 cup minced leek
3/4 cup minced zucchini
1 fresh garlic clove, minced
1 1/2 teaspoons sugar or to taste
Salt and freshly ground pepper
1 1/2 quarts (6 cups) chicken stock
1/2 cup whipping cream
freshly chopped parsley (garnish)

Melt butter in large stockpot over medium-high heat. Add onion and sauté 1 to 2 minutes. Reduce heat to low and add remaining ingredients except stock, cream and parsley. Cook until vegetables are soft but not browned, about 20-25 minutes.

Add stock and bring to boil over medium-high heat. Reduce heat and simmer about 10 minutes. Let cool slightly. Transfer to blender or processor in batches and puree until smooth. Taste and adjust seasoning. Return to stockpot, place over medium heat and gradually stir in cream. Heat through but do not boil. Garnish each serving with chopped parsley. Serves 6-8.

FOUR HOUR STEW

1 can beef broth
1 cup red wine
1 - 5 oz. Can tomato sauce
2 1/2 pounds stew beef, cut into "largish" cubes
6 Tablespoons tapioca
5 carrots, cut into pieces
2 red onions, and 1 yellow onion, cut into pieces
4 potatoes, cut into "largish" pieces
4 cups celery, cut julienne style
2 1/2 cups green peppers, cut in large chunks
1 bay leaf
2 cloves fresh garlic, minced
salt and pepper to taste (Lawry seasoned pepper is very good)

Do NOT brown beef. Place all ingredients in a very large casserole dish, placing seasonings and bay leaf on top. Cook at 300 degrees for 4 hours, covered. Do not peek! Serves 8.

GAZPACHO

1 cup finely chopped, peeled tomatoes
1/2 cup EACH finely chopped green pepper, celery and cucumbers
1/4 cup chopped onion
1 teaspoon snipped chives
2 teaspoons snipped parsley
1 small clove garlic, minced
3 Tablespoons tarragon wine vinegar
2 Tablespoons extra virgin olive oil
1 teaspoon salt
1/4 teaspoon freshly ground pepper
1 teaspoon Worcestershire® sauce
2 cups tomato juice

Combine all ingredients together in a glass or stainless steel bowl. Chill 4 hours or more before serving. Serve cold, in chilled bowls, garnished with fresh parsley sprigs.

HOLLY'S CABBAGE SOUP

1 medium green cabbage
1 medium yellow onion
1 extra large can tomato juice
5 beef bouillon cubes
Grated cheddar and Jack cheese

Core cabbage and cut into chunks. Slice whole onion into medium sized slices. Add cabbage, onion and bouillon cubes to tomato juice in a large kettle or pot. (You can add water if desired to reduce thickness of soup.) Bring mixture to a gentle boil then cover and cook, stirring occasionally, over low heat for 2 to 3 hours. Serve in bowls with freshly grated cheeses on top. This recipe also freezes quite well.

ICED LEMON SOUP

1 onion, chopped
1 clove garlic, crushed
3 Tablespoons butter
1/4 cup all-purpose flour
3 3/4 cups good quality chicken stock
grated zest (rind and juice) of 2 large lemons
salt and white pepper to taste
1 bay leaf
1 1/4 cups half and half (light cream)

Fry onion and garlic in butter until soft but not colored. Stir in flour and gradually add stock. Bring to boil. Add lemon rind and juice, seasoning and bay leaf. Cover and simmer 20 minutes. Remove bay leaf. Strain soup and place in a large bowl. Stir in half and half and adjust seasonings to taste. Cool, then chill thoroughly in refrigerator. Serve cold in chilled bowls, garnished with thin slices of lemon and a sprig of mint if desired. Serves 8-10.

LIL'S CLAM CHOWDER

6 slices bacon, cut up
1 can tomatoes (1 quart)
2 packages onion soup mix
1 tomato can of water
6 potatoes, diced

Fry bacon, drain off most of the fat. Add other ingredients and simmer 1/2 hour or until potatoes are tender. Add 1 quart minced clams and heat through. Add 1 to 2 cans milk and 1/2 teaspoon soda (or fresh milk, for curdling). Heat and serve. Do not boil. If mixture starts to curdle, add more milk.

MEATBALL SOUP

MEATBALLS:
1 pound lean ground beef
1 yellow onion, grated fine
1 fresh tomato, chopped fine
1/4 cup raw white rice
salt, pepper and Beaumonde seasoning to taste

SOUP:
1 quart chicken broth
1 - 16 oz. Can stewed tomatoes, cut up
1 yellow onion, chopped
3 stalks celery, sliced julienne style
3 carrots, slice julienne style
3 small or 2 medium zucchini, sliced
2 potatoes, cut into chunks

Combine meatball ingredients in large bowl, and using clean hands, shape into small balls (should make about 25-30).

Combine soup ingredients into large pot and cook slightly, bringing to a boil. Add raw meatballs, and let simmer until meatballs float to the top of the pot. At this point, you can let the soup simmer gently indefinitely, but you may need to add more liquid. Add salt, pepper and more Beaumonde if desired. Best if made a day ahead. This soup freezes well.

NEW ENGLAND CLAM CHOWDER

1/4 lb. Salt pork, diced
1 large yellow onion, finely chopped
1 cup boiling water
3 medium potatoes, diced
1 teaspoon salt

1/4 teaspoon pepper
2 ea. 8 oz. Cans minced clams
2 cups milk
1 cup light cream (Half and Half)
fresh parsley and thyme

Fry salt pork in skillet until brown and crisp; remove, drain. Sauté onion in remaining fat until golden and clear. Add water, potatoes, salt and pepper; cover, simmer until potatoes are tender. Add clams with liquid, heat. Add milk and cream and season to taste. Simmer gently until ready to serve; do not allow to boil. Serve in bowls topped with salt pork and dash of parsley and thyme. Serves 6.

ONION SOUP FONDUE

3/4 cup sweet butter
5 large yellow onions, thinly sliced
2 quarts beef broth (can also use water with beef bouillon cubes)
1 teaspoon chicken seasoned stock base
white pepper
Round loaf of French or sourdough bread, sliced 1" thick
Jack cheese slices (1 oz. Slices) - lots!
Garlic toast (see below)

In a large kettle, melt butter, add onions and sauté until onions are translucent but not browned. Add beef broth and chicken base. Cover and simmer 2 to 3 hours. Remove from heat and allow to stand overnight. Next day, remove and discard fat. Reheat and season to taste with pepper.

Meanwhile, lightly toast bread slices and top each with about 5 slices of Jack cheese. Place soup in ovenproof individual serving dishes and top with a bread slice. Run soup under broiler just until cheese bubbles and is soft, but not browned. Serve with garlic toast on the side. Makes 12 servings.

Garlic Toast: Spread bread slices with garlic-flavored butter and grated Parmesan cheese and toast lightly under broiler.

PUMPKIN, ORANGE & THYME SOUP

2 Tablespoons extra virgin olive oil
2 cloves fresh garlic, chopped fine
2 medium yellow onions, finely chopped
7 cups diced fresh pumpkin
6 1/4 cups boiling vegetable stock
finely grated rind and juice of 1 large orange
3 Tablespoons fresh thyme, leaves only
2/3 cup whole milk
salt and pepper

Heat the olive oil in a large saucepan. Add the onions to the pan and sauté for about 4 minutes, until softened. Add the garlic and pumpkin, and cook for another 2 minutes, stirring well. Add the boiling vegetable stock, orange rind and juice, and 2 Tablespoons of the thyme to the pan. Simmer, covered, for 25 minutes, until the pumpkin is tender. Place the mixture in a food processor or blender, and blend until smooth. (Or, you can mash the mixture by hand using a potato masher until smooth.) Season with salt and pepper. Return the soup to the saucepan and gradually add the milk. Reheat briefly for about 5 minutes until it is very hot, but not boiling. Sprinkle with the remaining fresh thyme and serve immediately in warm bowls. Serves 4.

SCOTCH BROTH

This soup also freezes extremely well.

2 lbs. Meaty beef soup bones
2 quarts water
7 whole peppercorns
1 1/2 teaspoons salt
1 1/4 cup chopped carrots
1/2 cup chopped turnips
1 1/4 cup chopped celery
1 1/4 cup chopped onion
1/4 cup medium pearl barley

In a large kettle, combine soup bones, water, peppercorns and salt. Cover and simmer for 2 1/2 hours, or until the meat comes easily off the bones. Strain broth; cool and chill. Skim off fat. Remove meat from bones, dice and return to broth along with remaining

ingredients. Bring to a boil. Reduce heat, cover and simmer about 1 hour or until vegetables and barley are tender. Makes about 2 quarts (6-8 servings).

SMOKEY'S TORTILLA SOUP

2 teaspoons virgin olive oil
1 (7-oz. Can) diced green chiles
2 cloves fresh garlic, minced
1 medium yellow onion, chopped
1 medium zucchini, chopped
1 large carrot, chopped
3 cups tomato juice
2 cups chicken broth
2/3 cup fresh cilantro
1 Tablespoon Worcestershire® sauce
1/2 teaspoon Tabasco® sauce
1 teaspoon chili powder
1 teaspoon ground cumin
1/2 teaspoon salt
5-6 flour tortillas, cut into strips
2 cups cooked, shredded chicken
1/3 lb. Monterey Jack cheese, grated
1/2 cup sour cream

Heat oil in large skillet or pot. Add chiles, garlic and onion. Cook, uncovered, over low heat until soft. Add zucchini, carrot, tomato juice, broth, Worcestershire® sauce, Tabasco® sauce, chili powder, cumin and salt. Mix well and bring to a boil; reduce heat and cook, uncovered, on low for 1 to 2 hours.

Preheat oven to 350 degrees. Place tortilla strips on cookie sheet and bake until crisp. Remove from oven and set aside. Add chicken to the hot soup and mix well; cook just long enough to heat chicken through.

Divide tortilla strips among four bowls and pour in soup. Top each bowl with cheese, sour cream, and cilantro. Makes 4 large servings.

30

SOUTHERN STYLE CORN CHOWDER

8 oz. Lean salt pork, diced
8 Tablespoons (1 stick) unsalted butter
3 large yellow onions, chopped
1 large green pepper, seeded and diced
8 medium potatoes, peeled and diced
4 cups milk
2 cups whipping cream
5 cups fresh corn kernels, or 5 cups thawed frozen kernels, cooked until tender
1/4 cup minced fresh parsley
Salt and freshly ground black pepper
Freshly grated nutmeg
Crisp-cooked bacon, crumbled (garnish)

Cook salt pork in large skillet over low heat until 2 Tablespoons fat have been rendered. Remove any remaining solid pork. Add 2 Tablespoons butter to skillet and let melt. Increase heat to medium, add onion and sauté until pale golden. Add green pepper and sauté briefly until just tender but still bright green. Remove from heat.

Cook potatoes in enough boiling salted water to cover until potatoes are tender but still hold their shape. Drain well.

Combine milk and cream in large saucepan and heat slowly. When hot, add remaining ingredients except butter and bacon. Bring just to simmer, then remove from heat and let stand at least 3 hours to cool and thicken. (Soup may be prepared to this point, covered and stored overnight in the refrigerator.) Just before serving, reheat soup gently. Carefully stir in remaining butter, being careful not to break or mash vegetables. Thin with milk if desired. Pass bacon separately to garnish each serving. Serves 12.

SPINACH SOUP
(Can be served hot or cold)

Thaw 2 packages frozen, chopped spinach, and press out as much liquid as possible. Sauté 1/2 onion (chopped) in 2/3 stick of butter; cook until onion is translucent.

Add enough all-purpose flour to make a roux. Add half and half to the desired consistency -- more half and half will make a thinner soup. Add salt and a large pinch of white pepper to taste while simmering. Add 6 sprigs fresh parsley to chopped spinach and puree in blender. Combine all ingredients and chill well in the refrigerator. If served cold, serve in chilled bowls with dollop of sour cream sprinkled with nutmeg on top. For warm version, heat soup (do not boil) and sprinkle nutmeg on top just before serving. This soup can also be frozen.

TOWNHOUSE CHEESE SOUP

4 small carrots, cut into 1" matchsticks
3 celery stalks, cut into 1" matchsticks
1 1/2 cups chicken stock
2 Tablespoons (1/4 stick) butter
2 Tablespoons finely chopped onion
1/4 cup all-purpose flour
3 cups hot chicken stock
1 cup shredded sharp Cheddar cheese
1 - 8 1/2 oz. Can whole tomatoes, undrained, chopped
10 drops Tabasco® sauce
1/8 teaspoon nutmeg
Salt to taste
1/4 cup dry white wine
1 1/2 cups whipping cream, heated
Popcorn or chopped parsley (garnish)

Add carrots and celery to 1 1/2 cups chicken stock in a 1 to 2 quart saucepan. Bring to boil, reduce heat and simmer until tender, about 15 minutes. Set aside.

Melt butter in a 4-5 quart saucepan over medium heat. Add onion and sauté until translucent but not brown. Add flour, blend well, and cook 5 to 7 minutes, stirring constantly so the mixture does not brown. Slowly, stir 3 cups hot chicken stock into flour mixture and cook over low heat, whisking constantly, until sauce thickens. Blend in cheese and stir until cheese melts. Add tomatoes and undrained vegetables. Season with pepper sauce, nutmeg, salt and wine. Just before serving soup, stir in hot cream. Garnish with popcorn or chopped parsley. Serves 6.

WEDDING BELL SOUP

Serves 10-12
BROTH:
1 - 5 lb. Stewing chicken, halved or cut into pieces
4 quarts water
6 plum tomatoes
4 celery stalks
4 parsley sprigs
2 large carrots
1 large onion
1 slice fresh ginger
1 teaspoon dill
1/4 cup chicken soup base or concentrate

MEATBALLS:

1/2 lb. Lean ground veal
1/4 cup Italian breadcrumbs
1 egg, lightly beaten
4 teaspoons grated Parmesan cheese
1 teaspoon minced parsley
1 small fresh garlic clove, minced
1/4 teaspoon freshly ground pepper
3 Tablespoons extra virgin olive oil

1/2 lb. Kale, spinach, escarole or curly endive, coarsely chopped

FOR BROTH: Place chicken in an 8-quart pot. Add water and bring to boil over high heat. Reduce heat to medium; skim fat off top. Add next 7 ingredients. Return to boil, cover and simmer over low heat about 3 to 4 hours. About 1/2 hour before chicken is done, stir in soup base. Remove chicken and reserve for another use. Cool broth slightly and strain. Refrigerate broth several hours or overnight. Remove solidified fat.

FOR MEATBALLS: Combine first 7 ingredients and form into 3/4" balls. Heat olive oil in large skillet over medium heat. Add meatballs and sauté until browned on all sides. Drain on paper towels.

FINAL PRESENTATION: Bring broth to boil over high heat. Reduce heat to low, add meatballs and simmer uncovered about 10 minutes. Add greens and cook 5 minutes. Serve immediately.

Meewowy Breads & Cereals

Kitties like to knead their dough!

"Dogs eat; cats dine." - Ann Taylor
"To err is human; to purr feline." - Robert Byrne

ANN'S SWEDISH RYE BREAD
(4 loaves)

Mix into a paste and let stand:
2 pkgs. Dry yeast
1 teaspoon granulated sugar
1 cup warm water (105 degrees)
1 1/2 cups white flour

Mix separately and scald:
2 cups milk with 1 cup water
Add: 5 Tablespoons oleo
1/2 cup molasses
1/2 cup brown sugar
3 Tablespoon dark Karo® syrup
1/4 cup white sugar
1 teaspoon caraway seed
4 teaspoons salt
1/2 teaspoon anise seed

Cool to lukewarm and add:
3 cups rye flour and 1 cup white flour

Mix well and add yeast mixture. Add 2 cups white flour. Mix and add 2 cups white flour again. Put 1 1/2 cups white flour on bread board. Dump rye mixture and knead in until flour is used up. Place in large, greased bowl, cover, and let rise in a warm place until doubled in bulk. Punch down and knead again, then make into 4 loaves and let rise in greased baking pans, covered, until double sized (use round cake pans for round loaves, and/or regular loaf pans). Bake at 325 degrees for 1 hour. Brush tops of warm loaves with butter.

AUNTIE TOM'S NUT BREAD

2/3 cup granulated sugar
1 cup nuts, chopped fine
1 cup milk
2 eggs
1 heaping teaspoon salt
3 1/2 teaspoons baking powder
3 cups all-purpose flour

Mix all ingredients together well, and put into a well greased pan. Let stand 20 minutes

before putting into the oven. Bake for 1 hour in a slow oven at 350 degrees.

BANANA BREAD

1/2 cup shortening (butter, oil, or Crisco®)
1/2 cup granulated sugar
1/2 cup brown sugar
2 eggs, beaten
4 ripe bananas, mashed
1/2 teaspoon salt
2 cups sifted flour
1 teaspoon baking soda
1/4 cup nuts, chopped fine

Cream shortening and sugars together, then add beaten eggs. Sift flour together with soda and salt, and add to wet mixture. Add nuts and mashed bananas, blending together until well mixed. Pour into greased loaf pan and bake for 1 hour at 350 degrees. Cool on wire rack.

CRACKED WHEAT BREAD
(Makes great cloverleaf rolls, too!)

1 cup cracked wheat
1 cup water
1 cup milk
2 Tablespoons granulated sugar
2 Tablespoons butter or margarine
2 teaspoons salt
2 cups whole wheat flour
1 envelope dry yeast
2 cups all purpose flour
1/2 cup soy flour
1/4 cup wheat germ
Cooking oil

In saucepan, bring cracked wheat and water to a boil. Remove from heat and stir in milk, sugar, butter and salt. Cool to 125 degrees or lukewarm. Mix whole wheat and soy flours with yeast. Add liquid mixture and wheat germ and beat until smooth, about 2 minutes at medium speed on mixer or 300 strokes by hand. Add 1 cup all purpose flour and beat 1 minute on medium speed of mixer or 150 strokes by hand.

Stir in more all purpose flour to make a moderately stiff dough. Turn onto lightly floured surface and knead 10 to 12 minutes. Shape into a ball and place in lightly greased bowl, turning to grease all sides. Cover and let rise in a warm place until doubled, about 1 1/2 hours. Punch down. Divide dough into thirds. Shape into balls and let rest, covered, 10 minutes. Place balls on greased baking sheets and roll into 1/2 inch circles. (For cloverleaf rolls, make 3 small 3/4 inch balls and put into greased muffin tins). Brush with oil. Let rise, covered, in warm place until doubled, about 45 minutes. Bake at 325 degrees 12 to 15 minutes, or until done.

CRANBERRY BREAD

1 cup granulated sugar
1 egg
2 cups all purpose flour
1/2 teaspoon baking powder
1/2 teaspoon salt
grated zest of 1 orange
2 Tablespoons butter, combined with enough water and the juice of 1 orange to yield 3/4 cup
1 heaping cup raw cranberries, sprinkled with
1 Tablespoon all purpose flour
1 cup finely chopped pecans

Cream egg and sugar together, then alternate adding liquid and dry ingredients to mixture. Add cranberries and nuts. Pour into greased loaf pan and bake at 350 degrees for 1 hour. Let sit for 24 hours before cutting. Freezes well.

DATE BREAD

1 cup chopped dates
1 cup boiling water
1 teaspoon baking soda
Soak above 3 ingredients together for 15 minutes.

3/4 cup granulated sugar
1 egg
Beat above 2 ingredients together well, then add to the date mixture.

1 1/4 cups all-purpose flour
1/4 teaspoon salt
1 Tablespoon melted butter
Add last 3 ingredients to mixture above. Pour into greased loaf pan and bake at 300 to 325 degrees at least 40 minutes, or until tester comes out clean.

FANCY CHERRY COFFEE CAKE

1 cup granulated sugar
1/2 cup butter, softened
1 cup sour cream
2 large eggs
1 teaspoon vanilla
2 cups all-purpose flour
1 1/2 teaspoons baking powder
1/2 teaspoon baking soda
1/2 teaspoon salt
1 - 21 oz. Can cherry pie filling

Topping:
1/4 cup all-purpose flour
1/4 cup granulated sugar
1/3 cup chopped pecans
2 teaspoons ground cinnamon
3 Tablespoons butter

Heat oven to 325 degrees. Combine 1 cup sugar and 1/2 cup butter in large mixer bowl. Beat at medium speed, scraping bowl often, until creamy (1 to 2 minutes). Add sour cream, eggs and vanilla; continue beating until well mixed. Reduce speed to low; add 2 cups flour, baking powder, baking soda and salt. Beat until well mixed (2 to 3 minutes).

Spread half of batter into greased and floured 13 inch by 9 inch baking pan. Spoon cherry pie filling over batter. Spoon remaining batter over pie filling; spread carefully.

Stir together 1/4 cup flour, 1/4 cup sugar, pecans and cinnamon in medium bowl. Cut in 3 Tablespoons butter until mixture resembles coarse crumbs. Sprinkle crumb topping mixture over batter. Bake for 45 to 50 minutes or until toothpick inserted in center comes out clean and topping is dark golden brown. Serves 15.

FANCY FRENCH BREAD

Halve one uncut long loaf of fresh Sourdough French Bread (to create a "top" and a "bottom")
1 cup mayonnaise
1 cup finely chopped yellow onion
1 large can diced green chiles
1 cup shredded cheddar cheese
1 cup shredded Jack or Swiss cheese

Mix together the above ingredients and spread evenly on the insides of the "top" and "bottom" slices of French bread. Wrap in foil and bake at 350 degrees until cheese has melted and the top of the loaf is turning golden brown, but is not burned. Cut into slices and serve warm.

GRANDMA'S CEREAL

1 cup almonds
1 cup pecans
1 cup cashews
1 cup filberts
1 cup oats
1 cup currants
1 cup wheat germ
1 cup brown sugar

Put all ingredients except for the currants into blender and blend to cereal consistency. Do not overblend. Add currants. Serve cereal with milk. I LOVED this as a little girl!!

HAROLD'S DOUBLE RISING TEXAS SCONES

1 package active dry yeast
2 teaspoons granulated sugar
1/2 cup warm water (105 degrees to 115 degrees)
1 1/4 cups unsifted all-purpose flour, divided
3/4 cups rolled oats
1 cup buttermilk
3 Tablespoons canola oil
2 Tablespoons baking powder
1/8 teaspoon baking soda
3/4 cup raisins
3/4 cup coarsely chopped fresh pecan halves

Mix the dry yeast and sugar together in a small bowl. Add the warm water and mix well until the yeast and sugar are dissolved. Set aside in a warm place so mixture will foam.

In a large mixing bowl, mix one cup of the flour and the rest of the dry ingredients. Use a fork and mix well. Add the canola oil and stir with the fork until the mixture appears to be coarse and grainy throughout.

Add the buttermilk and the foamy yeast mixture. Use a large mixing spoon and mix until a large ball is formed in the bowl. (You can use a dough mixing attachment in your mixing machine instead if you wish.) If the mixture seems a little moist and sticky, add some of the remaining flour until a ball can be formed.

Cover the mixture in the bowl and leave in a warm place (about 85 degrees F) for about an hour. The mixture should become about one and a half times the original size. Dust the top of the ball with a little flour and test with your fingers to see if the ball feels spongy. If not, let it rise for another half hour. Dust a cutting board with flour and roll the mixture onto the board. Dust your hands with flour and knead the mixture lightly, forming it into a ten inch pie-shaped circle. Cut the circle into eight pie slices and place on a cookie sheet, taking care to have the slices well spaced apart. Cover and let stand in a warm place for about an hour. Bake in a 400 degree oven for twenty minutes. Allow to cool about 10 minutes before eating. If you like a crispy brown top, brush the scones with an egg wash made by scrambling one egg with 2 Tablespoons of milk.

HOLIDAY ANISE BREAD

1 package active dry yeast
1/2 cup warm water (about 110 degrees)
1/2 cup warm milk
2 Tablespoons granulated sugar
1 1/2 Tablespoons anise seed
1/2 cup butter or margarine, melted
2 eggs
1/2 teaspoon salt
About 4 to 4 1/2 cups all purpose flour, unsifted
2/3 cup packed brown sugar
1/2 teaspoon ground cinnamon
Sugar Glaze (see below)

In a large electric mixer bowl, soften yeast in the warm water. Add the milk, granulated sugar, anise seed, 3 Tablespoons of the butter, eggs, salt and 1 1/2 cups of the flour. Beat at medium speed until smooth, about 5 minutes.

Using a heavy-duty mixer or a wooden spoon, gradually beat in the remaining 2 1/2 to 3 Cups flour to form a soft, elastic dough. Turn out onto a lightly floured board and knead until a smooth, non-sticky dough forms, about 6 minutes. Place dough in a greased bowl and turn to grease the top. Cover and let rise in a warm place until doubled, about 1 1/2 hours.

Punch down dough. On a lightly floured board, roll out into a 12 by 22-inch rectangle. Brush remaining 5 Tablespoons butter over dough to within a half inch of the edges. Combine brown sugar and cinnamon, and sprinkle evenly over the butter. Starting from a wide side, tightly roll up jelly-roll fashion, and pinch the edges to seal dough roll.

Pick up roll, being careful not to stretch it; place, seam side down, in a greased 10" tube pan. Pinch ends together to close circle of dough in the pan. Make 7 evenly spaced slashes 1/2" deep around the top of the dough roll to expose cinnamon layer. Cover dough in pan and let rise again in a warm place until doubled, about 45 minutes.

Bake in a 350 degree oven for 50 to 60 minutes, or until it sounds hollow when tapped and is lightly browned on top. Cool in pan 5 minutes then turn out on a wire rack. To serve warm from the oven, spoon on sugar glaze, letting it drizzle down sides. Toast individual slices to reheat. (If you make the bread ahead, cool thoroughly, then wrap until airtight. Reheat, wrapped in foil, at 350 degrees for about 20 minutes, then drizzle the glaze on top and serve. Makes 1 large loaf.

Sugar Glaze: Blend 1/2 Cup unsifted powdered sugar with 1 Tablespoon water until smooth.

JALAPENO CORN BREAD

3/4 cup all-purpose flour
2/3 cup granulated sugar
3/4 cup cake flour
1/2 cup yellow cornmeal
2 Tablespoons baking powder
1/2 teaspoon salt
3 large eggs
2/3 cup whole milk
1/3 cup buttermilk
1/4 cup corn oil
2 Tablespoons sour cream
3 Tablespoons butter, melted
1/4 cup red bell pepper, very finely chopped
1 jalapeno pepper, seeds and veins removed, very finely chopped

Heat the oven to 325 degrees. Butter and lightly flour a 13" x 9" baking pan. Place the all-purpose flour, sugar, cake flour, cornmeal, baking powder and salt in a large mixing bowl and stir well to combine. In another large mixing bowl, combine the eggs, milk, buttermilk, oil, sour cream, butter, bell pepper and jalapeno and stir well to combine. Add the wet ingredients to the dry ingredients and mix thoroughly. Pour the batter into the pan and bake until firm in the center and golden on top, about 30-35 minutes. Let cool

15 to 20 minutes before cutting into squares to serve. Makes 12 servings.

LEMON BREAD

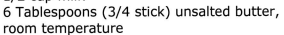

Makes 1 9" x 5" Loaf
1 cup granulated sugar
1/2 cup milk
6 Tablespoons (3/4 stick) unsalted butter, room temperature
2 eggs
1 1/2 cups all purpose flour
1 teaspoon baking powder
1 teaspoon salt
Finely grated zest (peel) of 1 large lemon (about 1 Tablespoon)
Lemon Glaze (see below)

Preheat oven to 350 degrees F. Grease and flour 9" x 5" loaf pan. Cream butter and sugar in mixing bowl, then add milk and eggs slowly. Mix well. Blend in dry ingredients and lemon zest. Turn into pan and bake for 1 hour at 350 degrees. Let cool slightly. Remove from pan and set on piece of foil. Pour hot Lemon Glaze slowly over surface. Let bread cool completely before slicing.

Lemon Glaze:
1/2 cup granulated sugar
1/4 cup fresh lemon juice

Combine ingredients in small saucepan. Place over low heat and stir until sugar dissolves and glaze is quite hot.

MACADAMIA NUT MUFFINS

2 1/2 cups cake flour
1 teaspoon baking powder
3/4 teaspoon salt
1 cup granulated sugar
2 large or 3 medium eggs
1/4 cup water
1/2 cup melted butter
1/2 cup finely chopped macadamia nuts

Sift together flour, baking powder and salt. Stir in sugar. Mix eggs and water and add all at once with melted butter to flour mixture.

Stir just enough to moisten dry ingredients. Fold in nuts. Place paper muffin cups inside muffin pan holes. Fill papers 2/3 full and bake at 350 degrees for 20 minutes. Makes 12 muffins.

MERK'S COFFEE CAKE

1/2 cup fat (butter, Crisco®, lard, etc.)
3/4 cup granulated sugar
1 teaspoon vanilla extract
3 eggs
2 cups sifted all-purpose flour
1 teaspoon baking powder
1 teaspoon baking soda
1/2 teaspoon salt
1/2 pint sour cream
6 Tablespoons butter
1 cup firmly packed brown sugar
2 teaspoons cinnamon
1 cup chopped nuts

Cream fat and sugar; add vanilla and eggs, 1 at a time. Beat well. Sift flour, baking powder and soda and add alternately with sour cream. Spread half of the batter in a 10" tube pan that has been greased and lined on bottom with waxed paper. Cream butter, brown sugar and cinnamon together - add nuts. Mix well. Sprinkle half the nut mixture evenly over batter in pan, then add the rest of the batter, and finish with the remainder of the nut mixture for topping. Bake in a 350 degree oven for 50 minutes.

MOTHER'S SOFT GINGERBREAD CAKE

1 cup granulated sugar
1 cup molasses
3/4 cup butter
1/2 teaspoon each ginger, cinnamon, ground cloves
2 teaspoons baking soda
2 1/2 cups all purpose flour
1 cup boiling water
2 eggs, well beaten

Dissolve baking soda in 1/2 cup of boiling water. Combine all ingredients except eggs and mix well. (There will be 1 cup boiling water total in cake.) Add the well beaten eggs to the mixture last thing before pouring into greased and floured 9" x 12" baking pan. Mixture will be quite thin. Bake at 350 degrees for 35 -40 minutes. (This recipe is my Great-Grandmother's!!)

ORANGE COFFEE CAKE

2 cups all-purpose flour
1 teaspoon baking soda
1 teaspoon salt
Sift above 3 ingredients together

1/2 cup Crisco®
1 cup granulated sugar
Cream above 2 ingredients together, then beat in 2 eggs, 1 at a time

Put through grinder:
1 medium orange
1 cup raisins (soaked overnight in orange juice with brandy)

Add grinded orange and raisins to egg mixture. Alternate adding the sifted ingredients and 1 cup milk at slow speed until all has been mixed together. Bake in a large oblong 9" x 13" Pyrex baking dish at 350 degrees for 30-35 minutes. Remove from the oven and drip the juice of one orange over the top while cake is still hot. Then, sprinkle 1/4 cup granulated sugar mixed with 1 teaspoon cinnamon and 1/2 cup chopped nuts.

POPOVERS

6 eggs
2 cups milk
6 Tablespoons margarine
2 cups all purpose flour, sifted well
1 teaspoon salt

About 1 1/2 hours before serving:
1. Preheat oven to 375 degrees
2. Grease (with butter) custard cups, and arrange in oblong baking pan

3. With mixer at low speed, beat eggs slightly, then beat in milk, butter, flour and salt just until blended (do not over beat)
4. Pour batter into custard cups within 1/4" of the top
5. Bake for 1 hour
6. Leaving baking pan on oven rack, carefully pull out rack part way and quickly slit the side of each popover to let out steam
7. Immediately return to oven and close door to continue baking about 10 more minutes
8. Promptly lift out each popover with fingers

PUMPKIN BREAD

3 1/2 cups sifted flour
1 1/2 teaspoons salt
3 cups granulated sugar
3/4 teaspoon cinnamon
3/4 teaspoon nutmeg
2 teaspoons baking soda
3/4 cup water
4 eggs
1 cup cooking oil
2 cups pumpkin (fresh, mashed, or canned)
1 cup chopped nuts

In a large mixing bowl, sift together flour, salt, sugar, cinnamon, nutmeg and soda. Make a well in the middle of the mixture and pour water, eggs, oil, pumpkin and nuts into the center of the well. Mix wet and dry ingredients well. Pour batter into 3 greased 7 1/2" x 5 1/3" loaf pans. Bake at 350 degrees for 1 hour, or until toothpick inserted in the middle of the loaf comes out clean.

REFRIGERATOR BRAN MUFFINS

1 quart buttermilk
2 cups All Bran®
1 cup butter
1 1/2 cups granulated sugar
4 eggs
4 cups bran buds
5 cups all purpose flour
4 teaspoons baking soda
1 teaspoon salt

Mix all ingredients together to make batter which can then be stored in the refrigerator for up to 6 weeks. When ready to make, pour batter into greased muffin tins and bake at 400 degrees for 16-17 minutes.

SOUR CREAM COFFEE CAKE

1 cup sour cream
2 eggs
1 1/2 cups all-purpose flour
1 cup granulated sugar
1/4 teaspoon salt
1/2 teaspoon baking soda
1/2 teaspoon baking powder
1 stick butter
sugar mixed with cinnamon

Beat sour cream and eggs. Combine dry ingredients and add to sour cream mixture. Beat until smooth. Spread batter into lightly greased 8" x 10" pan. Bake at 350 degrees for 25 minutes. While hot, rub with stick of butter until all is absorbed. Sprinkle top with mixture of sugar and cinnamon.

STRAWBERRY FRENCH TOAST

4 each 1 1/2 inch slices King's Hawaiian Sweet Bread®
2 cups sliced fresh strawberries
4 large eggs
1/2 cup milk
1/2 teaspoon vanilla
1/4 teaspoon nutmeg
1/4 teaspoon cinnamon
1/4 cup granulated sugar
1 teaspoon grated orange rind
Powdered (confectioner's) sugar
Warm maple syrup

Cut each slice into thirds. Using a serrated knife, cut a pocket in edge of each slice and fill with strawberries. Combine remaining ingredients. Quickly dip (do not allow to soak) slices in egg mixture. Cook on hot buttered or oiled griddle until golden brown on both sides. Sprinkle with powdered sugar and top with additional strawberry slices.

Serve immediately with warm syrup. Serves 4.

STUFFED ROLLS

1 dozen rolls (finger rolls), or soft French rolls split half way through on side. Remove part of the center of the roll to mix with filling.

Put through a grinder:
1 pound Tillamook cheese
1/2 pound minced ham
2 green bell peppers
1 yellow onion
1 small bottle stuffed olives

Add 1/4 pound melted butter, the roll crumbs, and 1/2 can tomato sauce.

Fill rolls and wrap in aluminum foil. Heat 30 minutes at 325 degrees.

VERMONT'S MAPLE OATMEAL BREAD

1 cup hot brewed coffee
3/4 cup boiling water
1/2 cup Vermont Maple syrup
1/3 cup vegetable oil
1 cup old-fashioned oats
1/2 cup granulated sugar
2 teaspoons salt
2 packages (1/4 oz. EACH) active dry yeast
1/4 cup warm water (105 degrees to 115 degrees)
2 large eggs, lightly beaten
5 1/2 to 6 cups bread flour

In a bowl, combine the first seven ingredients. Cool to 105 degrees to 115 degrees. Meanwhile, in a large mixing bowl, dissolve the yeast in warm water. Add the oat mixture, eggs, and 2 cups of the flour; mix well. Stir in enough remaining flour to form a soft dough. Turn onto a floured surface; knead until smooth and elastic, about 8-10 minutes. Place in a greased bowl, turning once to grease the top. Cover and let rise in a warm place until doubled, about 1 hour. Punch dough down. Turn onto a lightly floured surface; divide in half. Shape into loaves. Place in 2 greased 9" x 5" loaf pans. Cover and let rise again until doubled; about 30-45 minutes. Bake at 350 degrees for 40-45 minutes or until golden brown. Remove from pans to wire racks to cool. Makes 2 loaves.

ZUCCHINI BREAD

2/3 cup cooking oil
1 cup granulated sugar
2 eggs
1 cup grated, unpeeled zucchini
1 1/2 cups flour
1 3/4 teaspoons cinnamon
3/4 teaspoon baking soda

1/4 teaspoon baking powder
3/4 cup chopped nuts
3/4 cup raisins, plumped overnight in warm water

Blend oil and sugar together. Beat eggs into mixture one at a time. Place grated zucchini in a separate bowl. Fold egg mixture into the zucchini. Sift together flour, cinnamon, soda and baking powder. Gradually, add flour mixture, nuts and raisins to zucchini mixture and mix well. Pour batter into 2 greased 8" x 4" loaf pans. Bake at 325 degrees for 1 hour. Makes 2 loaves.

Catty Notes

Purry Good Vegetables

Our pick of the litter!

"A kitten is the rosebud
in the garden of the animal kingdom."
- Robert Southey

ASPARAGUS ALA GRILL

1 large bunch asparagus
extra virgin olive oil
salt and pepper
dash of fresh lemon juice
dash of grated Parmesan cheese
mayonnaise

Heat up the BBQ grill. While grill is heating, take a flat pie pan and pour in the olive oil to a depth of about 1/4 inch, sprinkling with salt and pepper and lemon juice. Cut off the very ends of the washed asparagus. Take the asparagus and carefully dip each stalk into the oil and lemon juice mixture, turning to coat all sides. Put asparagus on the BBQ on medium heat, closing grill and cooking about 10 minutes. Turn carefully with tongs, and cook another 10 minutes. Remove to a serving platter, sprinkle cooked vegetable with Parmesan cheese. Serve with mayonnaise for dipping.

BLEU CHEESE & ROSEMARY SCALLOPED POTATOES

5 pounds medium sized Russet potatoes
2 teaspoons salt
1/2 teaspoon freshly ground black pepper
2 teaspoons minced fresh rosemary
1 cup crumbled bleu cheese
1 cup grated Parmesan cheese
1 cup sour cream
2 cups heavy cream
1 teaspoon salt

Preheat oven to 350 degrees. Butter a 9" x 13" glass baking dish. Peel and slice the potatoes into 1/4 inch slices. Put them in a large bowl with the salt, pepper and rosemary. In a small bowl, toss together the cheeses. Layer half the potatoes in the buttered baking dish. Sprinkle with half the cheese mixture and top with the remaining potatoes. In a bowl, whisk together the sour cream, heavy cream and salt, and pour over the potatoes. Tap the baking dish on the counter to spread out the sauce and release

any air bubbles. Sprinkle top with remaining cheese mixture. Bake potatoes for about 1 hour and 20 minutes, or until browned and completely tender all the way through when poked with a knife. Serve immediately. Makes 12 servings.

BROCCOLI SPOON BREAD

1 bunch broccoli (about 1 1/2 pounds)
1 1/2 cups milk
1/2 cup yellow cornmeal
2 eggs, separated
2 teaspoons baking powder
1 teaspoon salt
1 Tablespoon granulated sugar
Parmesan cheese

Trim broccoli, cutting stems 2" long. Slit stems almost to florets if stalks are thick. Place broccoli in large saucepan with a small amount of boiling, salted water. Cover and cook until crisp-tender, about 5 minutes. Drain, reserving 1/2 cup liquid for sauce. Gradually stir milk into cornmeal and cook and stir over medium heat until thickened, about 5 minutes. Cool slightly. Beat egg whites until stiff but not dry. Fold into cornmeal mixture. Arrange broccoli in a well-greased, deep, 2 quart soufflé dish. Spoon batter over, smoothing to edges of dish. Bake at 375 degrees for 45 to 50 minutes, or until nicely browned. Serve warm with Parmesan Cheese Sauce (see below). Serves 4-6.

PARMESAN CHEESE SAUCE:

2 Tablespoons butter
1 Tablespoon cornstarch
1 cup milk
1 cup grated Parmesan cheese
1/2 cup broccoli liquid from above
1/2 teaspoon salt
1/2 teaspoon white pepper
1/2 teaspoon nutmeg

Melt butter in small saucepan. Stir in cornstarch to form a smooth paste. Gradually stir in milk. Over low heat, cook and stir until sauce comes to a boil and thickens. Cook, stirring constantly, about 3 minutes longer. Add cheese, a little at a time, stirring until melted. Stir in broccoli liquid, salt, pepper and nutmeg. Heat; serve warm.

CHEESE TOPPED SPINACH

1 - 6 oz. Jar marinated, drained artichokes
2 - 10 oz. Packages frozen leaf spinach, completely thawed
1 - 8 oz. Package cream cheese, softened
2 Tablespoons butter
4 Tablespoons milk
1/2 cup grated Parmesan cheese

Preheat oven to 350 degrees. Add a little salt to the spinach. Place artichokes in bottom of a greased, 1-quart baking pan. Drain spinach well and spread over artichokes. Blend cream cheese with butter and add milk slowly, mixing well. Spread cream cheese mixture over top of spinach, reaching all the way to the edges of the baking pan. Sprinkle top with Parmesan cheese. Cover and bake for 45 minutes. Remove cover and bake 10 minutes longer. Serves 6. Recipe can easily be doubled.

CHILE AND CHEESE BAKED RICE

1 cup white rice, cooked per package instructions and cooled
2 cups sour cream
Salt
1/2 pound sharp Cheddar cheese, shredded
2 - 4 oz. Cans diced green chiles
3 Tablespoons butter or margarine
1/3 cup grated Parmesan cheese

Combine rice, sour cream and salt to taste, mixing well. Spread half of rice mixture in a buttered 1 1/2 quart baking dish. Sprinkle half the Cheddar cheese on top. Add a layer of green chiles and top with remaining Cheddar cheese. Spread remaining rice on top. Dot surface with butter and sprinkle evenly with Parmesan cheese. Bake at 350 degrees for 30 minutes. Serves 6 to 8.

CRISPY POTATOES

4 medium russet potatoes, cut into large wedges
1 Tablespoon extra virgin olive oil
1/4 teaspoon freshly ground black pepper
1/8 teaspoon salt
2 fresh cloves garlic, minced (optional)
ketchup (optional)

Place potatoes in a large bowl; add cold water to cover. Let stand for 15 minutes. Preheat oven to 425 degrees. Spray a non-stick baking sheet with a vegetable cooking spray such as Pam®. Set aside. Drain potatoes in a colander. Spread on a double layer of paper towels. Press down on the towels to dry potatoes thoroughly. Transfer dried potatoes to a clean large bowl. Sprinkle with oil, pepper and salt; toss gently to combine. Arrange seasoned potatoes in a single layer on prepared baking sheet. Bake potatoes for 20 minutes. Using a spatula, carefully turn potatoes; sprinkle with garlic. Bake until golden, about 20 minutes, turning baking sheet after 10 minutes for even browning. Serve immediately with ketchup on the side if desired.

EGGPLANT & MUSHROOM CASSEROLE

3 eggplants, about 6 inches long, washed
salted water
1 cup minced onions
2 1/3 Tablespoons extra virgin olive oil
salt and pepper to taste
1 pound fresh mushrooms, washed and minced
butter
1 1/2 (3 oz.) packages cream cheese, softened
1/4 cup minced parsley
1/2 teaspoon basil
1/4 teaspoon thyme
3 Tablespoons shredded Swiss cheese
3 Tablespoons fine dry bread crumbs

Peel and slice eggplants. Soak in salted water to cover for 1 hour. Pour off water. Add clear water, cover and simmer until tender, about 30 minutes. Drain and place eggplant in mixing bowl.

Meanwhile, sauté onions in 1 1/2 Tablespoons olive oil in skillet about 10 minutes, or until tender but not browned. Season lightly with salt and pepper and add to eggplant in mixing bowl. Sauté mushrooms in 3 Tablespoons butter and remaining 1 Tablespoon oil until lightly browned, 5 to 6 minutes. Season to taste and add to eggplant mixture. Stir cream cheese slightly, then beat into eggplant mixture. Stir in parsley, basil and thyme.

Turn eggplant mixture into a 2 quart casserole and top with cheese and breadcrumbs. Sprinkle with 2 to 3 Tablespoons melted butter. Place casserole in another, larger, pan filled with 1 inch water, and bake at 375 degrees for 25 to 30 minutes. Serves 6-8.

GARLIC-Y BUTTER-Y GREEN BEANS

1 pound fresh or frozen green beans
1/2 cup sliced fresh mushrooms
6 Tablespoons butter
3 teaspoons onion powder
1 1/2 teaspoons garlic powder
salt and pepper to taste

Cook green beans in water to cover until tender. Meanwhile, in a skillet, sauté mushrooms in butter until tender. Add onion powder and garlic powder. Drain beans; add to skillet and toss. Season with salt and pepper. Serves 6.

GRANDMA'S LUSCIOUS POTATOES

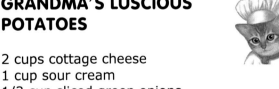

2 cups cottage cheese
1 cup sour cream
1/3 cup sliced green onions
2 teaspoons salt
1/4 teaspoon garlic salt
5 cups cold, diced potatoes (boiled, then allowed to cool and peeled when cooled)
1/2 cup shredded Cheddar cheese

Combine all ingredients in large mixing bowl and mix well. Turn into a lightly greased 1 1/2 quart casserole dish. Bake at 350 degrees for about 50 minutes, or until heated through and cheese has melted. Serves 4-6.

GREEN BEANS, SWISS STYLE

2 Tablespoons butter
2 Tablespoons all purpose flour
1 teaspoon salt
1/4 teaspoon freshly ground pepper
1/4 teaspoon granulated sugar
1/4 teaspoon grated yellow onion
1 cup sour cream
4 cups cooked French style green beans (or 2 packages frozen)
1/2 pound grated Swiss cheese
3/4 cup cornflake crumbs mixed with 2 Tablespoons butter

Melt butter; stir in flour, salt, pepper, sugar and onion. Add sour cream gradually, stirring constantly. Continue to cook and stir until mixture thickens. Fold in beans and pour into a buttered 1 1/2 quart casserole dish. Sprinkle grated cheese on top, then sprinkle with crumb mixture. Bake at 400 degrees for 30 minutes.

GRILLED CORN ON THE COB, TERIYAKI STYLE

1/2 cup butter, softened
1 Tbsp. Fresh ginger
1 Tbsp. Minced fresh garlic
2 Tbsp. Bottled Teriyaki sauce
1 Tbsp. Minced green onions
1 Tbsp. Minced fresh cilantro
1 tsp. Salt
1/2 tsp. Bottled red chile or Tabasco® sauce
8 ears white corn on the cob (carefully discard the corn silks without breaking off the corn husks)

Do not microwave the butter, but let it stand in bowl to soften. Add ginger, garlic, Teriyaki sauce, green onions, cilantro, salt and chile sauce to bowl and mix well. Pull back husk away from corn and spread butter mixture on outside of each ear of corn. Pull husk back over corn and tie ends together with butcher twine. Soak corn in ice water for 15 minutes. Drain the corn and grill over medium heat, turning occasionally (every 2-4 minutes) for approximately 30 minutes. Husks will become slightly charred, but not burned. Remove corn from grill, and let cool slightly. Remove and discard husks and serve. Serves 8.

JACK CHEESE VEGETABLE BAKE

2 Tablespoons corn oil margarine
1/2 pound fresh broccoli, broken into florets, stems peeled and cut into 1/2" pieces
1 1/2 Tablespoons soy sauce
1 1/2 teaspoons minced fresh garlic
1 teaspoon celery seed
1/2 teaspoon dried dill weed
Salt and freshly ground fine pepper
1/2 pound carrots, peeled and diced
1 small onion, diced
7 eggs
1 1/4 cups milk
1 pound Monterey Jack cheese, shredded

Melt margarine in medium skillet until foam subsides. Add broccoli stems and sauté briefly. Add soy sauce, garlic, celery seed, dill weed, salt and pepper. Cook over low heat about 5 minutes, stirring occasionally. Add carrots, onion, and broccoli florets; cover and cook until vegetables are tender, about 10 minutes, stirring occasionally.

Preheat oven to 350 degrees. Beat eggs and milk in large bowl. Add cheese and vegetables. Turn into lightly greased deep 3-quart baking dish. Place in large, shallow pan and add boiling water to depth of 1 inch. Bake until knife inserted in center comes out clean, about 55-60 minutes. Serves 8-10.

MARINATED MUSHROOMS

1 pound medium mushrooms
3/4 cup extra virgin olive oil
1 1/2 teaspoons grated lemon zest (peel)
1/4 cup lemon juice

1 teaspoon oregano, crushed
1 teaspoon garlic salt
1/8 teaspoon freshly ground black pepper

Cut mushrooms lengthwise into about 4 slices each (slices should be about 1/2 inch thick). Place in plastic bag or glass dish. Combine the test of the ingredients and pour over mushrooms. Seal plastic bag or cover the dish. Marinate mushrooms in liquid for at least 4 hours in the refrigerator, turning bag or stirring mixture occasionally. Drain liquid from mushrooms before serving. This marinade can then be saved and used for marinating other foods. Serves 12.

POTATO BEER CASSEROLE

4 large potatoes, peeled and sliced
2 large onions, sliced
2 cups sliced celery
all-purpose flour
1 cup beer (Imported beers are best; do not use light beer)
1 cup chicken stock
1 teaspoon salt
1/4 teaspoon white pepper
1/4 cup butter
1/2 cup dry bread crumbs
1/4 cup grated Parmesan cheese
1/4 teaspoon garlic powder
Paprika

Layer potatoes, onion and celery in a 2-quart casserole, sprinkling a small amount of flour between potato layers. Combine beer, chicken stock, salt and pepper and add to casserole. Cover and bake at 375 degrees 50 minutes to 1 hour, or until potatoes are almost tender. In saucepan melt butter and stir in crumbs, Parmesan cheese and garlic powder. Uncover casserole and sprinkle top with crumb mixture. Sprinkle overall with paprika for color and flavor, and bake, uncovered, an additional 10-15 minutes or until top is golden brown and potatoes are tender. Serves 8.

RAN'S TOMCATTIN' TOMATOES

3 large or 4 medium, firm red tomatoes
1/2 pint sour cream
1/2 teaspoon salt
1/4 teaspoon pepper
1 teaspoon granulated sugar
1 Tablespoon all-purpose flour
2 Tablespoons chopped green onion
2 Tablespoons canned chopped green chiles
1 cup shredded cheddar cheese

Cut out the tops of tomatoes (or slice the tomatoes thickly to make more servings). Arrange tomatoes on the rack of a broiler pan. Combine the other ingredients, except for the cheddar cheese, and stir until mixture is well blended. Spoon the mixture on top of the tomatoes, then sprinkle with the cheddar cheese. Place tomatoes in a preheated broiler about 4 inches from the heat and broil just until the cheese is bubbly and golden brown. Tomatoes will be just warm. Serves up to 8-9.

SAUTEED BELL PEPPERS

2 cloves fresh garlic, sliced thin
1 Tablespoon unsalted butter
1 Tablespoon extra virgin olive oil
1 red bell pepper, cut into 1/4" rings
1 yellow bell pepper, cut into 1/4" rings
1 orange bell pepper, cut into 1/4" rings
2 Tablespoons golden raisins, soaked in 1/4 cup boiling water for 15 minutes
2 teaspoons drained bottled capers, chopped coarsely
4 black olives, thinly sliced
2 Tablespoons pine nuts, toasted lightly

In large frying pan, sauté the garlic in butter and olive oil for 1 minute or until soft. Add pepper rings and sauté 1 minute more. Add raisins and their soaking liquid, capers and olives, and cook, covered, for 2 more minutes. Stir in pine nuts just before serving. Serves 2-4.

SAVORY POTATO CASSEROLE

8 medium red potatoes, boiled and cooled; unpeeled and grated
1/2 cup butter, melted with 2 chicken or beef bouillon cubes
2 cups sour cream
1/2 teaspoon salt
1/4 teaspoon finely ground black pepper
3 to 4 green onions, chopped
2 1/2 cups grated Cheddar cheese
1/2 cup crushed corn flakes

Melt butter with soup, sour cream, 1 cup cheese and onions. Add to grated potatoes with salt and pepper. Bake at 350 degrees for 30 minutes. Remove from oven and sprinkle the remainder of the cheese and the crushed corn flakes on top. Return to oven to continue baking for another 10 minutes. Let cool 5 minutes before serving.

SOUTHERN YAM AND ORANGE BAKE

3 pounds Louisiana yams
2 unpeeled oranges, sliced paper thin
1/2 cup brown sugar (packed firmly)
1/4 cup butter
1/2 cup California Muscatel, sweet sherry, or other dessert wine
1/4 cup strained honey
1/4 cup fine, dry bread crumbs
2 Tablespoons brown sugar
1 Tablespoon melted butter

Scrub yams well. Boil the yams in their jackets, covered, for 25-30 minutes or just until tender. Drain. When cool, peel and cut crosswise in thin slices.

Arrange alternate layers of yam slices and orange slices in a greased 2 quart casserole dish, finishing with a layer of yam slices on top. Sprinkle each layer with some of the 1/2 cup brown sugar, and dot with some of the 1/4 cup butter.

Mix wine and honey; pour over contents of casserole. Mix crumbs, the 2 Tablespoons brown sugar, and the 1 Tablespoon melted butter; sprinkle over the top. Cover and bake at 350 degrees for 50 minutes. Uncover casserole and return to oven for an additional 15 minutes to crisp the top.

STUFFED ZUCCHINI

1 large ("fat") 8 inch zucchini
2 Tablespoons butter
1 stalk finely chopped celery
1 green onion, finely chopped
2 water chestnuts
1/4 teaspoon parsley flakes
1/4 teaspoon dill weed
1 1/2 Tablespoon chili sauce
2 Tablespoons Parmesan cheese
6 crumbled saltine crackers
1 small jar spaghetti sauce

Wash and boil the zucchini in salted water for about 12 minutes. Split lengthwise and let cool. Scoop out center and chop.

In the 2 Tablespoons butter, sauté the rest of the ingredients with the exception of the Parmesan cheese, saltines and spaghetti sauce. Add the chopped and drained zucchini pulp to the mixture and blend well. Add the saltines. Divide the mixture and fill each zucchini half. Drizzle spaghetti sauce over top and sprinkle well with Parmesan cheese. Bake at 350 degrees for 25 minutes.

SWISS CHEESE BROCCOLI

1 pound broccoli, coarsely chopped
salt
3 Tablespoons butter or margarine
2 Tablespoons all-purpose flour
3 Tablespoons chopped onion
1 1/4 cups milk
2 cups shredded natural Swiss cheese
2 eggs, beaten
1/3 cup grated Parmesan cheese

Preheat oven to 325 degrees. Grease a 10" x 6" dish. In medium saucepan over high heat, heat broccoli and 1/2 teaspoon salt in 1" high water to boiling; cover and cook 10 minutes; drain and set aside.

Meanwhile, in medium saucepan over medium heat, melt butter; stir in flour and 1 1/2 teaspoons salt until smooth. Add onion and cook, stirring constantly, for 1 minute. Slowly stir in milk; cook, stirring constantly, until mixture thickens and begins to boil. Remove from heat.

Stir Swiss cheese and broccoli into mixture until cheese melts slightly; stir in beaten eggs. Pour into baking dish and sprinkle with Parmesan cheese. Bake 30 minutes at 325 degrees or until center is firm to the touch. Serves 8.

TOMATO PUDDING

3 cups cubed bread
3/4 cup melted butter
3/4 cup brown sugar, firmly packed
3/4 cup water
3/4 teaspoon salt
10 oz. Can tomato puree

Boil puree, sugar, water and salt for 5 minutes. Place bread in casserole. Pour butter over bread and boiled mixture over all. Bake at 350 degrees for 30 minutes.

YUMMY TOMATO BAKE

2 cups coarsely crushed unsalted soda crackers
1 cup shredded Cheddar cheese
1 medium yellow onion, minced
1/2 teaspoon salt
1/2 teaspoon granulated sugar
1 1/2 cups canned tomatoes
butter

Combine crackers, cheese and onion in layers in a well-greased casserole. Mix salt, sugar and tomatoes and pour over the cracker, cheese and onion layers. Dot with butter and bake at 350 degrees for 25 to 30 minutes. Serves 6.

ZUCCHINI WITH CORN

Put one inch layer of thinly sliced zucchini in a buttered casserole dish. Sprinkle with combination of 1/2 cup minced onion and celery; cover with fresh sliced tomato. Add a one inch layer of fresh corn (cut from the cob). Repeat layers to fill dish. Season with salt, freshly ground pepper, and sugar. Cover and bake at 325 degrees for 45 minutes.

"Cats are intended to teach us that not everything in nature has a purpose."
- Garrison Keillor

Sandy Spots

BLEU CHEESE STEAK WITH BUTTON MUSHROOMS

For the serious BBQ lovers out there!!
2 each large, 1" thick, fresh juicy steaks
(preferably Ribeyes or T-Bones - for best
results, have the butcher hand select them
for you)
1 1/2 cups spicy garlic marinade
salt and freshly ground pepper
3 oz. Crumbled bleu cheese, mixed with 2
coarsely chopped green onions
1 1/2 cups fresh button mushrooms, washed
well
1/3 to 1/2 stick butter
1 1/2 to 2 cups cooking sherry

Cover steaks in marinade and marinate
overnight in the refrigerator for best results.
About an hour before mealtime, melt butter in
a large heavy skillet, and add half the sherry.
Carefully, using a wooden spoon, add
mushrooms. Simmer on low heat, stirring
occasionally, for one hour, adding more
sherry as needed to keep moist and retain
some liquid. About 35 minutes before
mealtime, spray BBQ grill with Pam® non-
stick olive oil coating, then heat up the grill
by turning all burners on high heat. When
grill is ready and hot, reduce heat to medium.
Using tongs, carefully place steaks on the
grill, and season lightly with salt and pepper.
Cover grill, and cook for 8 minutes. Turn
steaks once, using tongs, and again sprinkle
lightly with salt and pepper. Top each steak
with bleu cheese and onion mixture. Cover
grill, and cook for another 8 minutes. Do not
over-cook!! Serve steaks on platter, and
pour mushrooms into a bowl with a large
spoon to pass around. Warm sourdough
French bread and a tossed green salad make
wonderful additions to this timeless favorite.
Serves 2.

BUTTERY BAY SCALLOPS

1 cup (2 sticks) butter, room temperature
1 cup fresh breadcrumbs
6 fresh garlic cloves, crushed
2 Tablespoons finely minced onion

1/2 cup chopped fresh parsley
1/4 cup white wine or Sherry
Juice of 1/2 lemon
Salt and freshly ground pepper

2 Tablespoons extra virgin olive oil
2 Tablespoons diced onion
1 1/2 pounds fresh bay scallops
1/2 pound fresh mushrooms, sliced

Mix together butter, breadcrumbs, garlic,
minced onion, parsley, wine, lemon juice and
salt and pepper. Form into roll and wrap with
waxed paper. Chill garlic butter until firm, at
least one hour.

Preheat oven to 450 degrees. Grease shallow
baking dish or au gratin pan. Heat oil in large
skillet over medium heat until haze forms.
Add diced onion and sauté until soft but not
browned. Add scallops and mushrooms and
salt and pepper to taste and sauté briefly.
Drain off liquid. Arrange scallop mixture in
prepared dish. Slice garlic butter and arrange
evenly over scallops. Bake until butter is hot
and bubbly, about 5 to 10 minutes. Serve
immediately. Scallops can also be broiled;
follow directions above but instead of baking
in the oven, turn on the oven broiler and
place the baking dish about 3 inches from
heat; broil until bubbly, about 3 to 5 minutes.
Makes 4 servings.

CHEESY LASAGNA

1 pound mild Italian pork sausage, casings
removed and meat crumbled or chopped
1 1/2 pounds lean ground beef
2 stalks celery, chopped
1 large yellow onion, chopped
1 large can (1 lb., 12 oz.) PLUS 1 small can
(14 oz.) Italian-style pear-shaped tomatoes
2 cans (6 oz. EACH) tomato paste
1/2 teaspoon salt
2 teaspoons oregano leaves
1/4 teaspoon pepper
1 package (10 oz.) lasagna, cooked and
drained according to package directions
Cheese filling (directions follow)
1 pound mozzarella cheese, thinly sliced

1/2 cup shredded Parmesan cheese

In a large saucepan or Dutch oven, combine sausage, ground beef, celery and onion, and cook on medium high heat, stirring frequently, until the meat is just beginning to brown and the vegetables are slightly soft. Add both cans of tomatoes and liquid, cutting the tomatoes into small chunks; add tomato paste, salt, oregano and pepper. Simmer uncovered, stirring frequently, for about 30 minutes, or until sauce is very thick. Remove sauce from heat and let stand undisturbed for about 10 minutes. Then spoon off and discard as much of the accumulated fat as possible. Spoon half the sauce into a shallow 3 1/2 to 4-quart casserole, spreading out evenly to edges of pan. Cover the sauce with an evenly distributed layer of half the cooked lasagna noodles. Spoon all of the cheese filling onto lasagna, spreading evenly to cover noodles. Cover with remaining lasagna noodles and top with the rest of the sauce, being careful to seal edges. At this point, you can cover and chill the casserole for later.

Bake, lightly covered with foil, in a 375 degree oven for 35 minutes (45-50 minutes if chilled) or until bubbling, then uncover and quickly arrange mozzarella slices over the surface, sprinkle with Parmesan cheese. Return casserole to the oven for 15 minutes to melt cheese. Let casserole stand about 5 minutes before cutting into rectangles. Serve with a wide spatula. Makes 8-10 servings.

CHEESE FILLING: Stir together 3 cups (1 1/2 pints) large curd cream-style cottage cheese or ricotta, 2 beaten eggs, 1/2 cup shredded Parmesan cheese and 2 Tablespoons minced fresh parsley.

CHICKEN FAJITAS (Barbequed)

4 skinless, boneless chicken breasts, marinated 24 hours in salad dressing marinade
1 small zucchini, coarsely chopped
1 small red onion, coarsely chopped
1/2 green bell pepper, finely chopped

4 Tablespoons extra virgin olive oil
salt and pepper to taste
fresh cilantro, parsley, sage and thyme, chopped
Fresh salsa
1 cup sour cream
8 flour tortillas

Spray BBQ grill with non-stick olive oil spray such as Pam®. Heat your BBQ with all burners on high for 15-20 minutes. Turn heat down to medium. Place chicken breasts on the BBQ and cook, covered, for 8 minutes. Turn once using tongs, sprinkle chicken lightly with salt and pepper, and cook an additional 8 minutes or until tender and cooked through. Do not over-cook. Meanwhile, add olive oil to a medium to large skillet, and sauté zucchini, onion, salt and pepper, cilantro, parsley, sage and thyme gently while chicken cooks. Add more oil if needed. When vegetables are tender but not soft, remove from heat; cover pan to keep warm. When chicken is done, remove from BBQ, let rest for about 10 minutes then cut julienne-style into about 1/2" thick strips. Place tortillas a couple at a time on the BBQ - they will cook quickly, so be prepared with your tongs to carefully turn them once when they are gently crispy, then place them on a serving plate. Serve chicken in a bowl; the tortillas on a plate; fresh salsa in a bowl; and the sour cream in a bowl. Each person will take their own tortilla and fill it with the ingredients of their choice, roll them up, and enjoy! Serves 4.

CHILE RELLENO CASSEROLE

1 - 7 oz. Can whole green chiles
3/4 pound Cheddar cheese, shredded
1/2 pound Jack cheese, shredded
4 eggs
2 Tablespoons all-purpose flour
1 can evaporated milk
1/2 teaspoon salt
1 - 6 oz. Can salsa (or use recipe for homemade salsa in this book)

Remove seeds from chiles and place half of them in a greased 9" x 9" baking pan. Sprinkle with half of both cheeses, add rest of chiles. Top with remaining cheeses. Beat eggs, flour, milk and salt together until smooth. Pour over casserole and bake at 350 degrees for about 30 minutes. Remove casserole from oven, pour on the salsa, and return to oven for an additional 25 more minutes. Serve warm. Serves 6.

CRAB LASAGNA

1/2 pound lasagna noodles
1 teaspoon extra virgin olive oil
2 - 10 oz. Cans cream of shrimp soup
2 - 8 oz. Cans crab meat, drained (or like amount frozen or fresh crab)
1 pint large curd cottage cheese
1 - 8 oz. Package cream cheese, softened
1 large yellow onion, chopped
1 beaten egg
1 teaspoon salt
2 teaspoons basil
1 cup grated Cheddar cheese

Cook noodles according to package directions, adding olive oil to boiling water. Rinse and drain very well. Combine shrimp soup, crabmeat, cottage cheese, cream cheese, onion, egg, salt and basil. Layer half of noodles in a 13" x 9" baking dish, spread with half the crab mixture, and sprinkle with half the Cheddar cheese. Top with remaining noodles, crab and Cheddar cheese, being sure to seal edges and cover all noodles. Bake at 350 degrees for 1 hour. Let stand about 15 minutes before cutting and serving. Serves 8.

CRAB WELLINGTON

1 pound fresh or frozen crab
2/3 cup chopped celery
1/4 cup chopped green pepper
1/4 cup finely chopped yellow onion
1 Tablespoon butter
1 - 10 1/2 oz. Can condensed cream of shrimp soup
1/3 cup chopped pimento-stuffed olives
2 cups biscuit mix
1 egg
1 Tablespoon water
Shrimp-Dill sauce (see below)

Slice crab. Sauté celery, green pepper and onion until limp in the butter. Add 1/3 cup cream of shrimp soup, reserving the remaining soup. Stir in crab and olives. Prepare biscuit mix according to package directions. Reserve small portion of the dough for leaf decoration. Roll remaining biscuit dough into 12"x9" rectangle. Spread with crab mixture and roll, jelly-roll style. Place on baking sheet, seam side down. Beat egg and water together. Shape reserved biscuit dough into leaves and decorate roll, attaching with egg mixture. Brush roll with remaining egg mixture. Bake at 400 degrees 25 to 30 minutes or until golden brown. Slice and serve warm with Shrimp-Dill sauce. Makes 6 servings.

SHRIMP-DILL SAUCE:

Reserved cream of shrimp soup
1/4 cup milk
2 teaspoons lemon juice
1/4 teaspoon dill weed

Combine remaining cream of shrimp soup with milk, lemon juice and dill weed. Heat, stirring frequently, until sauce is smooth and hot.

DOROTHY'S FETA & ARTICHOKE PIZZAS

1 small (or large) jar marinated artichoke hearts
1/2 to 1 cup fresh diced tomatoes
1/2 to 1 cup Pizza Sauce, canned or in jar
1 individual package of 2 Boboli® crusts
4 oz. Feta cheese, crumbled
2 Tablespoons Parmesan cheese
dash salt and pepper
pinch of oregano and thyme

Preheat oven to 400 degrees. Drain and quarter artichoke hearts. Spread crusts with pizza sauce, then top with artichoke hearts, tomatoes and Feta cheese. Sprinkle salt, pepper, oregano, thyme and Parmesan cheese on top. Bake for 8-10 minutes. Serve as individual pizzas. (Amount of ingredients above depends upon how many people are being served.)

DOUBLE RICE AND MEAT CASSEROLE

1 pound fresh mushrooms, sliced
1 small yellow onion, finely chopped
1/2 pound lean pork, cut into 1" cubes
1/2 pound lean beef, cut into 1" cubes
1/4 cup (1/8 lb.) butter
1/2 cup uncooked wild rice
1/2 cup uncooked white rice
4 Tablespoons (1/4 Cup) soy sauce
2 cups sliced celery
1 - 10 1/2 oz. Can mushroom soup
1/2 cup water
2 teaspoons freshly chopped rosemary
2 teaspoons freshly chopped thyme
Sprigs fresh parsley

Sauté mushrooms, onion, and meat cubes in butter until meat is lightly browned through; turn mixture into a 3-quart casserole. Wash wild rice well and add to meat mixture along with white rice. Add the soy sauce, celery, mushroom soup, rosemary, thyme and water; mix well. Cover and bake in a moderately slow oven (325 degrees) for 1 hour and 45 minutes. Garnish with fresh parsley. Serves 8.

EASY CHICKEN & BROCCOLI BAKE

2 - 10 oz. Packages frozen, chopped broccoli
1 - 10 3/4 oz. Can Cream of Mushroom soup
2 large eggs, beaten well
1 1/2 cups grated sharp Cheddar cheese
2 Tablespoons chopped onion
1 cup mayonnaise
2 large boneless chicken breasts (3/4 pound), cooked and diced
1/2 cup finely grated Parmesan cheese
salt and pepper to taste

Steam the broccoli until tender, about 10 minutes; set aside. Heat oven to 375 degrees. Combine the soup, eggs, cheese, onion, mayonnaise and chicken. Place half the broccoli in a 9 inch square baking pan or casserole dish and pour half the soup mixture

over the top. Layer the remaining broccoli over the top, then pour the rest of the soup mixture over it to form 2 layers. Sprinkle with salt and pepper, and top with Parmesan cheese. Bake until golden brown, 35 to 40 minutes. Serves 6.

EGGPLANT PARMESAN (Serves 10-12)

4 eggplants
Oil for frying
2 pounds (32 oz.) Cheddar cheese, shredded
2 pounds (32 oz.) mozzarella cheese, shredded
30 small-medium mushrooms, sliced
3 medium yellow onions, diced
12 oz. Tomato paste
5-6 small cans tomato sauce
3 eggs, beaten
white corn meal
Marjoram, thyme, rosemary, sage, oregano, sweet basil
Parmesan cheese

Slice eggplants thinly, dip in beaten egg batter, then coat with white cornmeal and fry in large skillet until crust turns light brown. Set aside. In large saucepan, combine mushrooms, onions, tomato paste, tomato sauce and all the spices, and gently heat through, stirring constantly to blend flavors. Layer large greased casserole dish with eggplant, sauce and then the shredded Cheddar and mozzarella cheeses, sprinkling each layer with Parmesan cheese. Repeat layers. Bake covered at 350 degrees for 1 hour.

FANTASTIC FETA CHICKEN

6 boneless, skinless chicken breast halves
2 Tablespoons lemon juice
2 teaspoons chopped fresh oregano or 1/4 teaspoon dried crushed oregano leaves
1/4 teaspoon ground black pepper
1 - 4 oz. Package crumbled Feta traditional cheese

Heat oven to 350 degrees. Place chicken in 9" x 13" baking dish. Drizzle with 1 Tablespoon of the lemon juice, then sprinkle with the oregano and pepper. Top with Feta cheese and drizzle again with the remaining 1 Tablespoon lemon juice. Bake 45 minutes or until cooked through.

FURBULOUS FILET MIGNON (WITH A CABERNET-SHALLOT SAUCE)

8 filet steaks, cut 1 inch thick
2 cups Cabernet wine
6 shallots, finely chopped
2 cloves fresh garlic, crushed
2 bay leaves
1 tsp. Freshly cracked black pepper
Salt and regular black pepper to taste

1 tsp. Extra virgin olive oil
1 cup beef broth
2 Tbsp. Butter
1 Tbsp. White flour
2 Tbsp. Fresh parsley, chopped

In a shallow glass dish, combine wine, shallots, garlic, bay leaves and cracked pepper. Add steaks, covering them with marinade. Refrigerate at least 6 hours, or overnight.

Remove steaks from marinade (reserving marinade), pat dry with a paper towel, and sprinkle with salt and pepper. Heat olive oil in a large sauté pan over high heat; carefully add steaks. Sear well, about 3 minutes on each side, until they reach an internal temperature of 145 degrees or higher, depending upon how well done you prefer your steaks.

Remove steaks from pan and transfer to a plate. Add remaining marinade, stir in the broth, and let reduce to 2 cups. In a small bowl, knead together butter and flour. Add to sauce a little at a time, whisking constantly. Bring sauce back to a boil; stir in parsley. Place steaks on serving plates and drape with sauce. Serves 4.

GRILLED SWISS GRUYERE SANDWICHES

8 slices potato-rosemary (or other soft white herbed) bread; sliced about 1/2 inch thickness
4 Tablespoons melted butter
6 oz. Swiss Gruyere, thinly sliced

For each sandwich, place slices of Gruyere between two slices of bread. Place under heavy cutting board and leave for 10 minutes. Brush one side of sandwich with butter and place butter-side down on griddle or in frying pan, over low-to-medium heat. When bread is golden brown, butter the top, flip sandwich and repeat browning the second side. Cut in half and serve hot. Serves 4.

HAWAIIAN QUICHE

1 - 9" frozen deep dish pie shell
1 - 8 oz. Can crushed pineapple in juice
4 oz. Sliced cooked ham
4 oz. Sliced process Swiss cheese
4 oz. Sliced sharp Cheddar cheese
1/4 cup chopped green pepper
1/4 cup chopped yellow onion
4 large eggs
1/2 cup Half and Half cream
4 teaspoons Dijon mustard
1/4 teaspoon horseradish
1/4 teaspoon beef stock base
1/4 teaspoon white pepper
pinch salt

Turn pineapple into a wire strainer to catch the juice, which you want to save. Measure 1/2 cup juice -- press pineapple with back of fork if needed to create more juice. Partially bake pie shell at 375 degrees for 10 minutes. Meanwhile, cut ham and cheeses into julienne strips. Melt 1/8 cup butter in a heavy skillet, then add onion and green pepper and cook slowly 4 minutes. Add the 1/2 cup pineapple juice and cook 4 more minutes or until liquid is absorbed. Add pineapple and ham strips and stir over heat just long enough to blend well. Spread mixture over bottom of pie shell, reserving 1/4 cup for the topping. Add cheese in separate clumps to vary the color inside the quiche.

Beat together eggs, Half and Half, mustard, pepper, horseradish, beef stock base and salt. Pour slowly into pie shell. Sprinkle remaining ham mixture on top. Dot with remaining 1/8 cup butter. Bake quiche at 375 degrees 30 to 40 minutes, or until set and lightly browned. Serves 4.

HERBED COTTAGE CHEESE ON RYE SANDWICHES

1 - 16 oz. Container low fat cottage cheese
1 Tablespoon minced fresh dill
1 Tablespoon minced fresh tarragon
2 Tablespoon snipped chives
1/4 teaspoon salt
dash white pepper
8 slices dark rye toast

Combine the cottage cheese, dill, tarragon, chives, salt and white pepper in a small bowl. Spread about 1/4 cup of the cottage cheese mixture on each slice of warm toast. If desired, sprinkle lightly with alfalfa sprouts. Serves 8.

HONEY-MUSTARD CURRY CHICKEN

2 1 1/2 to 2 lb. Broiler-fryer chickens, cut up
1/2 cup butter, melted
1/2 cup honey
1/4 cup prepared mustard
1 teaspoon salt
1 teaspoon curry powder

Place chicken pieces in shallow baking pan, skin side up. Combine butter, honey, mustard, salt and curry powder, and mix well. Pour mixture over chicken and bake at 350 degrees for 1 1/4 hours, basting every 15 minutes until chicken is tender and nicely browned. Serves 4-6.

LONDON BROIL

2 to 2 1/2 pounds trimmed flank steak
Meat tenderizer
3/4 cup canned tomato sauce
1/4 cup molasses
3 Tablespoons water
2 Tablespoons plus 1 teaspoon vinegar
1 Tablespoon extra virgin olive oil
1 Tablespoon instant minced onion
1 Tablespoon Worcestershire® sauce
1 1/2 teaspoon mustard
1 1/2 teaspoon salt
1/8 teaspoon freshly ground pepper
pinch of cayenne

Treat the meat with tenderizer according to jar directions. Mix remaining ingredients for sauce. Preheat broiler - lay flank steak in broiler pan and pour sauce over meat. Broil for 5 minutes, basting once, then turn beef over to broil another 5 minutes, with occasional basting. Check for the doneness you desire. Carve into thin slices, a little on the diagonal, and add sauce (pan drippings) to each serving. Serves 4.

MANGO HALIBUT

4 small to medium fresh halibut steaks (about 4 oz. Each)
salt and pepper to taste
2 Tablespoons butter
1/2 cup prepared mango chutney
1/4 cup fresh lime juice
1/4 cup slivered fresh basil
lime wedges for garnish

Rinse fish and pat dry; season both sides with salt and pepper. Melt butter in a large skillet; add fish. Cook over medium-high heat for about 5 minutes per side, or until fish reaches an internal temperature of 150 degrees F and flakes easily when tested with a fork. Add chutney, lime juice and basil; cook for 2 minutes more, turning fish once. Garnish with lime wedges and serve on colorful bed of greens. Serves 4.

MUSHROOM CRUST QUICHE

5 Tablespoons butter, divided
8 oz. Fresh mushrooms, coarsely chopped
1/2 cup finely crumbled saltine crackers
1/4 cup chopped green onions
2 cups shredded Monterey Jack cheese
1/2 pint small curd cottage cheese
3 large fresh eggs
1/4 teaspoon Paprika
1/4 teaspoon ground red pepper

Preheat oven to 350 degrees. In a large frying pan, melt 3 Tablespoons butter over medium heat. Add mushrooms and cook for 6 minutes (or until soft). Stir in crackers, then pour mixture into a well-greased 9 inch pie pan. Press evenly over bottom and sides to form crust.

In a small saucepan, melt remaining 2 Tablespoons butter over medium heat; add onions and cook over medium heat for 5 minutes (or until soft). Spread over crust and sprinkle evenly with Jack cheese. In a blender, combine cottage cheese, eggs and pepper until smooth. Pour into crust and sprinkle with Paprika. Bake, uncovered, for 25-30 minutes, or until a knife inserted just off-center comes out clean. Let stand 15 minutes before cutting into wedges for serving. Serves 4-6.

OVEN-FRIED SOLE FILLETS

2 large eggs
3/4 cup grated Parmesan cheese
2 Tablespoons all-purpose flour
4 sole fillets, preferably fresh (6 oz. Each)
3 Tablespoons extra virgin olive oil
3 Tablespoons butter
1/2 cup finely chopped salted, roasted macadamia nuts
Watercress or parsley sprigs
Lemon wedges

Heat oven to 425 degrees. Put a 10"x15" baking pan in oven to heat. In a 9" or 10" pie pan, beat eggs to blend. On a piece of waxed paper, mix cheese and flour. Dip fish in egg to coat, drain off excess, and coat in cheese mixture. Set fish in a single layer on waxed paper. Remove heated pan from oven; add oil and butter and swirl until butter melts. Lay a piece of fish in pan; turn to coat with butter. Repeat with remaining fish, setting slightly apart in pan. Sprinkle fish evenly with nuts. Bake, uncovered, in the 425 degree oven until fish is opaque in thickest part (cut to test), 8 to 10 minutes. With a wide spatula, transfer fish to serving platter. Garnish with watercress and lemon wedges. Serves 4.

RISOTTO WITH PRAWNS & ARTICHOKES

7 -8 cups chicken stock
2 tsp. Extra virgin olive oil
2 cloves fresh garlic, chopped
1 cup white rice
1/2 pound small prawns, peeled and cleaned (about 26-30 prawns)
8 oz. Frozen artichoke hearts
1 tsp. Lemon zest (finely grated lemon peel)
1 Tbsp. Fresh lemon juice
10 fresh basil leaves, cut in small pieces
sea salt and freshly ground black pepper

Heat stock in a 2-quart saucepan and keep warm. Heat olive oil in a large skillet; add garlic and sauté for 10 seconds. Add the rice and sauté for another minute, stirring constantly. Add 1 ladle of stock while stirring rice, until most of the liquid is absorbed. Continue adding the stock in the same way for 15 minutes, until the rice is done. (Rice will be tender and creamy with a slight crunch in the center.) Add the prawns, artichoke hearts, and lemon zest. Cook for 3 minutes. Remove from heat and stir in lemon juice and basil. Season with sea salt and pepper. Serves 4-6.

SALMON LOAF

1 - 15 1/2 oz. Can salmon, drained and flaked
2 cups soft bread crumbs
1/4 cup finely chopped yellow onion

1/4 cup finely chopped fresh parsley
4 large eggs, lightly beaten
1 Tablespoon Worcestershire® sauce
1 Tablespoon lemon juice
3/4 teaspoon salt
2 Tablespoons butter or margarine, melted
Tangy Cream Sauce (see below)

In a large mixing bowl, combine all ingredients (except Tangy Cream Sauce) and mix well with clean hands. Spoon into a greased loaf pan and spread smooth. Bake at 350 degrees about 45 minutes. Let stand for 5 minutes before un-molding on platter. Serve hot (preferably) or cold, with Tangy Cream Sauce.

TANGY CREAM SAUCE:

1 cup mayonnaise
2/3 cup milk
4 teaspoons lemon juice
2 teaspoons prepared mustard
2 teaspoons Worcestershire® sauce
1/4 teaspoon salt
Combine all ingredients in a medium saucepan and heat gently until sauce is hot but not boiling. Or, combine and serve cold over cold salmon loaf. Makes about 1 1/2 cups.

SAUTEED RED SNAPPER

2 - 8 oz. Fresh red snapper fillets
Milk
Flour seasoned with salt, pepper and garlic powder
1/2 cup clarified butter
4 Tablespoons fresh lemon juice
12 Tablespoons dry white wine
2 Tablespoons capers, drained

Cover fish with milk and let stand in refrigerator at least 4 hours. When ready to cook, preheat oven to 375 degrees. Remove fish from milk and dust lightly with seasoned flour. Heat butter in 12" ovenproof skillet over medium high heat. Add fish and sauté until brown on both sides. Remove from skillet and keep warm. Reduce heat, add lemon juice and wine to pan juices and simmer about 1 minute until ingredients are

well blended. Return fish to skillet and bake about 5 minutes or until fish flakes easily. Transfer fish to heated plate and sprinkle with capers. Makes 2 servings.

SAUTEED SALMON STEAKS

1 Tablespoon butter or margarine, melted
1 1/2 teaspoons soy sauce
1/4 teaspoon garlic powder
1 Tablespoon extra virgin olive oil
1 teaspoon crushed fresh rosemary
2 thawed salmon steaks
4 slices lemon

Combine butter, soy sauce, garlic powder and rosemary. Heat oil in medium skillet, add salmon steaks, and baste with butter mixture. Cook about 5 minutes or until browned, then turn. Continue basting with butter sauce and place lemon slices on steaks. Cook until salmon flakes when tested with a fork. (Note: this recipe works great on a barbeque grill, also!)

SCRUMPTIOUS LIVER

6 thick slices bacon
1 1/2 pounds baby beef liver, cut into serving sized pieces
all-purpose flour
1 large yellow onion, sliced
1 medium green bell pepper, seeded and sliced
1 envelope dry onion soup mix (enough for 4-6 servings)
1 - 1 pound can stewed tomatoes
seasoned salt and pepper

Fry bacon until crisp in wide frying pan over medium heat. Drain bacon on paper towels; reserve pan drippings. Return 2 Tablespoons drippings to pan. Dredge liver in flour and shake off excess. Fry liver in drippings until well browned on both sides, adding more drippings to pan if needed. Arrange liver in 9" x 13" baking dish.

Add onion and bell pepper to frying pan and cook until onion is limp; spoon vegetables evenly over liver, then sprinkle with onion soup mix. Pour stewed tomatoes over all. Sprinkle with seasoned salt and pepper, and top with bacon. Cover and bake at 350 degrees for 25 minutes or until heated through.   Serves 6.

SHRIMP ENCHILADAS

1/4 pound butter
1 medium stalk celery, diced
2 large onions, diced
1/2 bunch fresh cilantro, chopped
1 teaspoon salt
1 teaspoon white pepper
1 teaspoon garlic powder
1 teaspoon oregano
1 teaspoon marjoram
1 teaspoon ground coriander
1 1/2 pounds medium shrimp, cleaned and cooked
3/4 cup dry cooking sherry
12 (8 inch) flour tortillas
Extra virgin olive oil
Savory Salsa (see below)
Shredded Jack cheese
Guacamole or avocado slices
1 cup sour cream

Melt butter in a heavy skillet. Add celery, onions, cilantro, salt, pepper, garlic powder, oregano, marjoram and coriander, and sauté quickly. Just before vegetables are tender, add shrimp and sherry, bring to a boil, then remove quickly from heat.

Dip tortillas one at a time into hot oil to soften. Place some of the shrimp filling in center of each tortilla and roll to form an enchilada. Place seam side down in baking pan. Continue until all tortillas are filled and rolled, and place close together in the baking pan. Top with 4 cups or more Savory Salsa. Sprinkle generously with Jack cheese and bake at 450 degrees until cheese melts, about 7 minutes. Garnish with small dollop of sour cream and avocado slices or small dollop of guacamole. Makes 12 enchiladas.

SAVORY SALSA (for Shrimp Enchiladas):

1 large onion, cut into thin strips

2 1/2 Tablespoons shortening or lard
2/3 cup crushed canned tomatoes
2 cups diced canned tomatoes
1/3 cup canned tomato sauce
3 medium Anaheim chile peppers, peeled and chopped
Cilantro sprigs, chopped
Salt and white pepper to taste
1 teaspoon garlic powder
1/2 teaspoon ground thyme
1 teaspoon ground coriander
1 teaspoon paprika
1 2/3 cups water
1/3 cup flour

Cook onion in shortening in saucepan until translucent. Add crushed and diced tomatoes, tomato sauce, chiles, cilantro, salt, pepper, garlic powder, thyme, coriander, paprika and 2 cups water. Stir well and bring to a rolling boil. Blend flour with 2/3 cup warm water. Beat well to remove lumps or strain. Add to boiling mixture and cook, stirring frequently until blended and thickened. Makes about 5 1/3 cups sauce.

SHRIMP SCAMPI

3/4 lb. Raw shrimp, medium size, shelled and de-veined
6 Tablespoons butter
1 Tablespoon green onion, minced
1 Tablespoon extra virgin olive oil
5 fresh cloves garlic, minced or pressed
2 teaspoons lemon juice
1/4 teaspoon salt
2 Tablespoons minced fresh parsley
1/4 teaspoon grated lemon zest (peel)
Dash Tabasco® sauce
1/2 cup finely sliced mushrooms
Lemon Wedges

Pat shrimp dry on paper towel and set aside. In a wide frying pan, melt butter over medium heat. Stir in onion, mushrooms, oil, garlic, lemon juice and salt; cook until bubbly.

Add shrimp to the pan and cook, stirring occasionally, until shrimp turns pink (about 5 minutes). Blend in parsley, lemon zest, and Tabasco® sauce. Turn into serving dish. Garnish with lemon wedges. Serves 2.

SMOKED SALMON & ZUCCHINI QUICHE

8-inch pie dish
6 oz. Puff pastry dough
3 large whole eggs
1 medium zucchini, sliced in 1/4 inch rounds
10 oz. Heavy cream
dash of extra virgin olive oil
dash of minced fresh garlic
1 teaspoon fresh chopped rosemary
6 oz. Smoked salmon
2 oz. Parmesan cheese, freshly grated
salt and freshly ground pepper to taste

Preheat oven to 360 degrees. Roll puff pastry dough flat, then set into pie pan, fluting edges on the sides. In a medium saucepan, brown zucchini in olive oil, add garlic, and sauté until tender, about 5 minutes. Whisk eggs and cream in a bowl until blended, then season with salt, pepper, and rosemary. Flake salmon evenly across pie dish, add zucchini, cover with egg mixture, and sprinkle with cheese. Bake for 15 -20 minutes, or until center is firm, then let cool for 15 minutes before cutting. Best served with a fresh green tossed salad. Serves 4-6.

SOUR CREAM HAMBURGERS

1 pound lean ground beef
1/2 cup finely chopped yellow onion
1/3 cup sour cream
1/4 cup fine dry bread crumbs
1 teaspoon Worcestershire® sauce
1/2 teaspoon EACH salt and dry basil
1/4 teaspoon pepper
Sour Cream Sauce (See Below)
2 English muffins, split and toasted
3 thinly sliced green onions

In a medium sized mixing bowl, combine the beef, onion, sour cream, crumbs, Worcestershire®, salt, basil and pepper. Mix well with clean hands. Form into 4 round patties, each about 1 inch thick. Arrange patties on a rack in a broiler pan and broil 3 inches below heat for 5 minutes. Turn patties over and broil 5 minutes longer or until meat is done to your liking when slashed in the middle. (Patties can also be barbequed on medium high heat - cook 6 minutes on each side.)

Meanwhile, prepare sour cream sauce. Arrange each patty on a muffin half; spoon sauce evenly over top and garnish with sliced green onion. Makes 4 servings.

SOUR CREAM SAUCE: In a small pan, stir 1 teaspoon all-purpose flour into 2/3 Cup sour cream until smooth. Dissolve 1 beef bouillon cube in 1/4 cup hot water and gradually stir into sour cream mixture. Add 2 Tablespoons thinly sliced green onion, 1 Tablespoon chopped fresh parsley, and pepper to taste. Place over medium heat until gently heated through; stir several times. Add 1/4 cup crumbled bleu cheese just before serving.

SPAGHETTI ALA RICOTTA CHEESE

3 Tablespoons extra virgin olive oil
3 Tablespoons butter
12 oz. Dried spaghetti
3 Tablespoons chopped fresh parsley
1 cup freshly ground almonds
3/4 cup ricotta cheese
1/4 teaspoon each nutmeg and cinnamon
3/4 cup plain unflavored yogurt
1/2 cup hot chicken stock
salt and pepper
fresh parsley for garnish

Bring a large pan of lightly salted water to a full boil. Add the spaghetti and 1 Tablespoon of the olive oil and cook until tender, but still firm to the touch. Drain the water from the pasta, then toss the pasta with the butter and chopped parsley; set aside in a warm place. To make the sauce: mix together the ground almonds, ricotta cheese, nutmeg, cinnamon, and unflavored yogurt over low heat to form a thick paste. Stir in the remaining oil, then gradually stir in the hot chicken stock, stirring constantly, until smooth. Season sauce with salt and pepper to taste. Transfer the spaghetti to a warm serving dish, pour the sauce on top, and toss together well using two large forks and carefully lifting the pasta

SWISS HAM PIE

PASTRY: Sift together 1 1/2 cups sifted all-purpose flour and 1/2 teaspoon salt. Cut in 1/2 cup shortening. Sprinkle 1 Tablespoon cold water over mixture at a time, using a total of 4 to 6 Tablespoons water as needed. Form into a ball.

2 Tablespoons butter or margarine
2 Tablespoons all-purpose flour
1/8 teaspoon nutmeg
1 1/2 cups milk
4 oz. Shredded Swiss cheese
4 oz. Sliced aged Swiss cheese
4 large eggs
1 cup diced cooked ham

Roll pastry out on lightly floured board and fit into 9 or 10" pie plate; flute edges with finger or fork; brush with one beaten egg. In medium saucepan melt butter, then blend in flour and nutmeg. Add milk all at once; cook and stir until thick and bubbly. Add cheese -- stir till melted. Cool slightly; add ham and 3 eggs. Stir well. Pour into pastry shell. Bake in moderate oven at 375 degrees for 25 to 30 minutes. Trim with slices of Swiss cheese cut into triangles and arranged on top of pie. Let pie cool 10 minutes before cutting into wedges. Serves 6.

toward the center of the bowl to coat thoroughly. Serve hot with sprigs of parsley for garnish.

ZUCCHINI BEEF MEDLEY

2 pounds lean ground beef
salt and pepper
2 Tablespoons extra virgin olive oil
2 stalks celery, thinly sliced
1 large onion, diced
1/2 medium sized green pepper, seeded and diced
1/4 pound mushrooms, sliced
1 clove fresh garlic, minced or mashed
3 medium-sized zucchini, thinly sliced
1 can (1 lb. 12 oz.) whole tomatoes
2 Tablespoons fresh lime juice
1/2 teaspoon EACH ground cumin and basil leaves
1 teaspoon oregano leaves
3 teaspoons cornstarch blended with 1/4 Cup cold water
Shredded Parmesan cheese
Cooked rice: (we recommend combination of brown, white and wild rice)

Season ground beef with salt and pepper; shape into tiny meatballs, using about 1 Tablespoon meat for each. Brown quickly over high heat in the oil in a large skillet. Set meatballs aside. Discard all but 2 Tablespoons of the pan drippings. In the skillet, heat the drippings if needed and add the celery, onion, green pepper, mushrooms and garlic. Cook over medium heat, stirring, until the onion is translucent. Add zucchini, tomatoes with liquid (cut up the tomatoes into smaller pieces), lime juice, cumin, basil, oregano, and salt and pepper to taste.

Add meatballs, bring to a boil, then reduce heat and cover. Simmer about 5 minutes or until zucchini is tender. Stir cornstarch and water mixture into sauce and boil, stirring constantly, until sauce is thickened. Sprinkle Parmesan cheese on top and serve immediately over cooked rice.

Magnificat Desserts

The purr-fect finale!

"If there is one spot of sun spilling onto the floor,
a cat will find it and soak it up."
- Jean Asper McIntosh

ANGELIC CHOCOLATE DESSERT

1 - 12 oz. Package of chocolate chips
2 Tablespoons sugar
3 eggs, separated
1 pint whipping cream
1 Angel Food cake

Melt chocolate chips in top of double boiler, then add sugar. Remove front heat. Add unbeaten egg yolks; stir and cool for 5 minutes. Beat egg whites. Beat whipped cream. Add egg whites to chocolate mixture, then add the whipped cream. With clean hands, separate the cake into very small bite-sized pieces (3/4" x 3/4"), and place the pieces in the bottom of an 8" x 12" x 2" pan. Spread a layer of the chocolate mixture over the top of the cake pieces, then repeat layers. Keep in refrigerator and serve cold. This recipe also freezes well.

BEST YETS (Cookies)

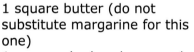

1 square butter (do not substitute margarine for this one)
1 cup crushed graham crackers
1 cup shredded coconut
1 - 6 oz. Package Nestlé's® chocolate chips
1 - 6 oz. Package butterscotch chips
1 cup chopped nuts
1 can Eagle Brand® condensed cream

Preheat oven to 350 degrees. Melt 1 square butter in 13" x 9" baking pan. Sprinkle graham cracker crumbs over/into the melted butter, then coconut. Sprinkle the rest of the ingredients as layers, then drizzle the condensed cream over the top of all. Bake for 1/2 hour at 350 degrees. Refrigerate at least an hour then cut into squares. These also freeze well.

BROWNIE PIE

3 egg whites
dash of salt
3/4 cup granulated sugar
3/4 cup finely crushed chocolate wafer crumbs
1/2 cup chopped nuts
1/2 teaspoon vanilla extract
Whipped cream sweetened with some granulated sugar

Beat egg whites and salt until soft peaks form. Gradually add sugar, beating until stiff. Fold in the chocolate wafer crumbs, chopped nuts and vanilla, then spread evenly in lightly buttered 9" pie plate. Bake in slow oven at 325 degrees for 35 minutes. Let cool. Spread top with whipped cream. Chill 3 to 4 hours, then top with shaved chocolate before serving.

CHEESECAKE COOKIES

1/3 cup butter
1/3 cup brown sugar
1 cup flour
1/2 cup chopped nuts
1/4 cup granulated sugar
1 each 8 oz. Package cream cheese
1 egg
2 Tablespoons milk
1 Tablespoon lemon juice
1/2 teaspoon vanilla extract

Cream the butter and brown sugar together until fluffy. Add the flour and nuts, blend until crumbly. Set aside 1 Cup of this mixture. Press remaining mixture into an 8" square pan and bake at 350 degrees for 12 minutes. Meanwhile, combine granulated sugar and cream cheese and beat until smooth. Add egg, milk, lemon juice and vanilla, and beat well. Spread over baked crust, and sprinkle the reserved crumbs on the top. Bake cookies at 350 degrees for 25 minutes. Cool, then cut into squares. These freeze very well.

CHOCOLATE CARAMEL BARS
(Cookies)

50 light caramels
1/3 cup evaporated milk
1 - 6 oz. Package chocolate chips

1 box Pillsbury® German chocolate cake mix
3/4 cup butter, melted
1 cup chopped nuts
1/3 cup evaporated milk

Melt caramels and 1/3 cup milk in top of double boiler. Grease and flour a 13" x 9" baking pan. Mix cake mix with butter, 1/3 cup milk and nuts. Spread half the dough into pan. Bake at 350 degrees for 6 minutes. Remove from oven and sprinkle with chocolate chips. Spread caramel mixture over the top. Use the remainder of the dough on top of caramel layer. Bake at 350 degrees for 15-18 minutes. Refrigerate at least an hour before cutting into squares. Keep refrigerated.

CHOCOLATE MINT DESSERT

2 cups vanilla wafers, crushed
1/4 cup melted butter
1/2 cup butter
1 1/2 cup sifted powdered sugar
3 eggs, lightly beaten
3 squares unsweetened baking chocolate, melted
1 1/2 cups whipping cream
1 package 8 oz. Miniature marshmallows
1/2 cup peppermint stick candy, crushed well
1 small package miniature semi-sweet chocolate chips

Blend vanilla wafer crumbs and melted butter, then press firmly on bottom of 8" square baking pan. Cream the butter and sifted powdered sugar together well. Add eggs and melted chocolate, and beat mixture until light and fluffy. Spoon over crumbs. Set in freezer to chill while whipping the cream. Gently fold miniature marshmallows and chocolate chips into whipped cream and spread over chocolate layer. Sprinkle the crushed peppermint candy on top for garnish. Serves 12 to 16.

CHOCOLATE NOODLE COOKIES

2 - 6 oz. Packages butterscotch chips
2 - 6 oz. Packages chocolate chips
2 - 3 oz. (Or 1 - 5 1/2 oz.) can chow mein noodles
1/2 cup cashews, halved or pieces

Melt (in the top of a double boiler) both types of chips together over boiling water (turn off heat so the chocolate melts without cooking - stir constantly). Stir in noodles, add nuts and mix quickly to coat each noodle. Drop by Tablespoon onto waxed paper and put into refrigerator to cool and set.

COCONUT CRUNCH TORTE

1 cup crushed graham crackers
1/2 cup moist shredded coconut
1/2 cup chopped nuts
1 Tablespoon powdered instant coffee
3/4 cup (semi-sweet or milk chocolate) chocolate bits or chips
4 egg whites
1 cup granulated sugar
1 teaspoon vanilla extract
salt

Beat egg whites, add sugar, vanilla, coffee and pinch of salt. When stiff, fold in remaining ingredients. Bake in 9" greased pie pan for 30 minutes at 350 degrees. Serve with coffee ice cream or whipped cream flavored with coffee. Serves 8.

EASY CHOCOLATE PEANUT BUTTER FUDGE

1 pound, 4 ounces dark chocolate
1/4 cup sweet butter
1/4 cup crunchy peanut butter
14 oz. Can sweetened condensed milk
1 teaspoon vanilla extract

Lightly grease an 8" square baking pan. Break the chocolate into pieces and place in a large saucepan with the butter, peanut butter, and condensed milk. Heat gently, stirring constantly until the chocolate, butter and peanut butter melt and the mixture is smooth. Do not allow to boil. Remove from the pan and the heat. Beat in the vanilla extract, then beat the mixture for a few minutes allowing it to thicken. Pour it into the prepared pan and level the top. Cover well and store in a cool, dry place for up to one month. This recipe does not freeze well.

FROZEN MOCHA CHEESECAKE

1 1/4 cup chocolate wafer crumbs (24 cookies)
1/4 cup granulated sugar
1/4 cup melted butter or margarine
1 - 8 oz. Package softened cream cheese
1 - 14 oz. Can Eagle Brand® condensed milk
2/3 cup chocolate syrup
2 Tablespoons instant coffee
1 teaspoon hot water
1 cup whipping cream, whipped

Combine wafer crumbs, butter and sugar for crust. Pat onto bottom and sides of buttered 13" x 9" baking pan. Chill. In large bowl, beat cream cheese till fluffy. Add Eagle Brand® condensed milk and chocolate syrup. Blend well. In small bowl, dissolve instant coffee in hot water, then add to first mixture and blend. Fold in whipped cream. Pour into prepared pan, cover, and freeze for 6 hours or until firm. Garnish with more crumbs or shaved chocolate. This can be made well in advance. Return leftovers to freezer immediately.

GIBBER'S SOUR CREAM CAKE

1 package Betty Crocker® Chocolate Fudge Cake Mix
1 package Betty Crocker® Creamy White Frosting
1 pint Sour Cream
2 eggs

3/4 cup water
1 teaspoon vanilla extract
1/4 cup margarine
1 square semi-sweet baking chocolate

Add 2/3 cup of the sour cream to dry frosting mix in small mixer bowl and chill. In large mixer bowl, blend 3/4 cup sour cream, the cake mix, eggs, water and vanilla. Beat 4 minutes at medium speed. Pour into 2 - 9" square cake pans and bake at 350 degrees for 25 to 35 minutes. Cool.

Add 1/4 cup soft margarine to sour cream-frosting mix. Blend, then beat on low speed for 1 minute. Do not over beat!! Spread frosting between cake layers and on the top and sides. Garnish with shaved chocolate. Keep refrigerated; use fairly large platter.

GOODIE COOKIES

1 heaping Tablespoon peanut butter
1 - 6 oz. Package chocolate chips (1 cup)
1/2 cup finely chopped nuts
1 1/2 cups Rice Krispies®

Melt chocolate in top of double boiler. Add peanut butter. Stir well. Remove from heat and add Rice Krispies® and nuts. Drop by teaspoonful on baking sheet covered with waxed paper. Put in refrigerator to harden. They will be ready to eat in about 15-20 minutes.

GRANDMA'S SUGAR COOKIES

1 cup powdered sugar
1 cup granulated sugar
1 cup butter
1 cup cooking oil
1 Tablespoon vanilla extract
2 eggs

Mix above ingredients together, then add 4 Cups plus 4 Tablespoons flour, 1 teaspoon baking soda, 1 teaspoon salt and 1 teaspoon cream of tartar. Mix well. Drop by rounded teaspoonfuls on lightly greased cookie sheet. Mash down with the bottom of a glass dipped in granulated sugar. Bake at 350 degrees for 12-15 minutes. Makes about 7 dozen cookies; recipe can be halved easily. Chill the dough for easier handling.

GRASSHOPPER PIE

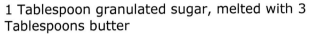

Crust:
2/3 package of chocolate wafers
1 Tablespoon granulated sugar, melted with 3 Tablespoons butter

Add the melted sugar and butter to the wafers, then pat inside the bottom and sides of a 9" pie pan. Bake at 350 degrees for 7 minutes, then let cool.

Filling:
In the top of a double boiler: Melt 24 large marshmallows with 1/4 cup milk. Stir well till blended, then let cool. Add 2 Tablespoons white crème de cacao and 3 Tablespoons green crème de menthe. Whip 1 cup whipping cream till stiff. Carefully fold the whipped cream into the marshmallow mixture. Pour into pie shell and chill in refrigerator.

HOLLY'S CARROT CAKE

3/4 cup butter or margarine
2 1/4 cups firmly packed brown sugar
3 eggs
4 1/2 cups coarsely shredded carrots (about 6 large)
2 2/3 cups regular all-purpose flour, unsifted
1 Tablespoon baking soda
2 teaspoons ground cinnamon
3/4 teaspoon salt
1 teaspoon ground nutmeg
3/4 cup chopped nuts

Cream Cheese Frosting: In a small bowl, cream together 3 oz. Cream cheese and 1/2 cup soft butter or margarine.   Add 4 cups sifted powdered sugar, 1 teaspoon vanilla and 1 Tablespoon grated orange peel; beat until creamy.

In a large bowl, beat together the butter and brown sugar until well blended, then add eggs, one at a time, beating well after each addition until creamy. Stir in carrots. Stir together the flour, baking soda, cinnamon, salt and nutmeg; stir into butter mixture. Fold in the nuts. Pour into a greased and floured 10" Bundt pan. Bake at 350 degrees for 55 to 60 minutes, or until a wooden toothpick inserted in the center comes out clean.

Cool in pan on rack for 15 minutes. Invert cake onto wire rack to cool completely. When cooled, spread cream cheese frosting evenly over top and allow to drip over sides of cake. Refrigerate any leftovers. Makes 10-12 servings.

KAHLUA MOUSSE

1 envelope unflavored gelatin
1/2 cup granulated sugar
1/2 teaspoon salt
1 cup milk
1 - 6 oz. Package semi-sweet chocolate pieces (1 Cup)
1/4 cup Kahlua
1 teaspoon vanilla
1 cup whipping cream, whipped

Mix gelatin, sugar and salt in a 2 1/2 quart saucepan. Stir in milk and chocolate pieces. Place over medium heat, stirring constantly, until the gelatin dissolves and the chocolate pieces melt. Remove pan from heat and beat with rotary beater until chocolate is blended. Stir in Kahlua and vanilla. Chill, stirring occasionally, until the mixture mounds slightly when dropped from a spoon. Fold in whipped cream. Turn into a 4-Cup mold (Pyrex bowl or soufflé bowl will do) and chill until firm. To serve, spoon into individual bowls and garnish with shaved chocolate and/or small mound of whipped cream.
Serves 6.

LEMON BARS (Cookies)

First layer:
1 cup all purpose flour
1/2 cup butter, melted
1/4 cup granulated sugar
pinch of salt

Second layer:
3 eggs, beaten
juice and grated zest of 1 1/2 lemons
1 1/2 cups sugar
3 Tablespoons all purpose flour
3/4 teaspoon baking powder

Frosting:
1 1/4 cups powdered sugar
1 teaspoon vanilla
2 Tablespoons butter
2 teaspoons milk

Mix ingredients for first layer together and press into bottom of a 9" x 13" baking pan. Bake at 325 degrees for 15 minutes.

Mix eggs with remaining ingredients for second layer and pour onto crust. Bake at 325 degrees an additional 20 minutes. When second layer is cooled and set, mix the frosting.

Mix frosting ingredients together well by electric mixer or by hand. This is a thin spreading frosting. Frost top of lemon bars and chill in refrigerator for at least an hour before cutting into 48 squares.

LEMON MERINGUE PIE

Filling:
4 large egg yolks
1/4 cup cold water
1/4 cup cornstarch
1 1/2 cups hot water
1 cup granulated sugar
1/2 cup fresh lemon juice
2 Tablespoons (1/4 stick) unsalted butter, cut into small pieces
1 Tablespoon grated lemon zest
Meringue:
4 large egg whites
1/4 teaspoon cream of tartar
pinch of salt
6 Tablespoons granulated sugar

1 - 9" pie crust, baked

For Filling:
Beat yolks until light and frothy. Combine cold water and cornstarch and mix until smooth. Combine cornstarch mixture, hot water, granulated sugar and lemon juice in top of double boiler over gently simmering water. Cook, stirring constantly with whisk, until sugar is dissolved and mixture is SLIGHTLY thickened. DO NOT BOIL! Remove from heat and begin adding yolks (drop by drop at first, to avoid any curdling), beating constantly until well blended. Again, place pan over gently simmering water. Gradually add butter, beating constantly with whisk until melted and mixture is smooth. Add lemon zest and continue cooking over low heat, stirring constantly, for 10 minutes. Remove from heat, cover, and let cool completely.

For meringue:
Beat egg whites until foamy. Add cream of tartar and salt and continue beating until soft peaks form. Gradually add granulated sugar, beating constantly, until stiff peaks form.

Assembly:
Preheat oven to 325 degrees. Pour cooled custard filling into crust. Spoon meringue evenly over top, spreading to all edges to cover and seal filling completely. Bake for 15-20 minutes, or until meringue is slightly browned. Cool to room temperature. Chill one hour before serving. Keep leftovers in the refrigerator. Serves 6-8

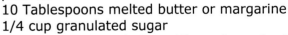

MARGARITA PIE

1 1/4 cup finely crushed pretzels
10 Tablespoons melted butter or margarine
1/4 cup granulated sugar
1 - 14 oz. Can Eagle Brand® condensed milk
1/3 cup ReaLime® lime juice (or the equivalent amount in squeezed fresh limes)

2 to 4 Tablespoons tequila
2 teaspoons triple sec
1 cup (1/2 Pint) whipping cream, whipped

(additional whipped cream, fresh mint leaves
or pretzels for garnish - optional)

Combine pretzel crumbs, butter and sugar.
Press firmly on bottom and sides of lightly
buttered 9" pie plate. In large bowl, combine
Eagle Brand®, lime juice, tequila and triple
sec, and mix well. Fold in whipped cream.
Pour into prepared crust. Freeze until firm
(about 4 hours). Garnish as desired. Re-
freeze leftovers.

MOON BALLS (Cookies)

2 cups honey
2 cups crunchy style peanut butter
4 cups nonfat dry milk (not instant)
4 cups crushed granola cereal such as Grape
Nuts Flakes®

Mix honey and peanut butter, add dry milk
slowly and mix well. Oil hands and form the
mixture with palms into small 3/4" round
balls. Roll in crushed flakes (or, you can add
the crushed flakes to the mixture before
forming into balls). Chill at least 1/2 hour in
the refrigerator before serving. Keeps well in
refrigerator.

NEVERFAIL PIE CRUST

3 cups all purpose flour
1 teaspoon salt
1 1/2 cups Crisco®
1 egg
4 Tablespoons water
1 Tablespoon vinegar

Use ingredients that are cold. Cut the dry
ingredients into the wet ingredients with a
pastry cutter or two forks until the size of
small peas. Roll out on board, then fit into
pastry or pie dish. Brush crust with the white
of one egg to avoid sogginess. Bake crust
unfilled at 450 degrees for 10 minutes, then
turn down to 350 degrees and continue

baking, watching closely, until nicely brown
and toothpick inserted in middle comes out
clean.

NO-BAKE CHEESECAKE

1 envelope unflavored gelatin
1/4 cup boiling water
2 - 8 oz. Packages cream cheese, softened
1/2 cup sugar
1 cup vanilla yogurt
1 prepared graham cracker crust

Dissolve gelatin in boiling water. In a
separate bowl, use hand mixer to blend
cream cheese and sugar until smooth. Fold in
yogurt and gelatin. Spoon into piecrust and
refrigerate for at least 3 hours. Serve plain,
or try topped with fresh fruit.

OATMEAL RAISIN COOKIES

1/2 cup butter or margarine
1/2 cup granulated sugar
1/2 cup light brown sugar, firmly packed
1 egg
1 cup all purpose flour
1/2 teaspoon salt
1/2 teaspoon baking soda
1 cup chopped raisins
1 1/2 cup oatmeal
3 Tablespoons orange juice

Cream butter with sugars until creamy, then
add egg and beat again. Sift the flour with
the salt and baking soda. Gradually add dry
ingredients to butter mixture, alternating with
orange juice. Stir in raisins and oatmeal; mix
well. Cover and refrigerate overnight. Drop
by rounded Tablespoon on lightly greased
cookie sheet. Bake at 350 degrees about 15
minutes until lightly browned. Do not over
bake.

PEANUT BUTTER LAYER CAKE

1/2 cup butter, softened
1 1/4 cups granulated sugar
3/4 cup peanut butter chips, melted

2 eggs
1 teaspoon vanilla extract
2 cups all-purpose flour
1 teaspoon baking soda
1/2 teaspoon baking powder
1/2 teaspoon salt
1 1/2 cups plus 2 Tablespoons whole milk

Peanut Butter Frosting
1 cup peanut butter chips, melted
1 - 8 oz. Package cream cheese, softened
1 teaspoon vanilla extract
1/8 teaspoon salt
3 cups confectioner's (powdered) sugar
3 Tablespoons milk

In a large mixing bowl, cream butter and sugar until light and fluffy. Add melted peanut butter chips; mix well. Add eggs, one at a time, beating well after each addition. Beat in vanilla. Combine the flour, baking soda, baking powder and salt; add to creamed mixture alternately with milk. Pour into two greased and floured 9" round baking cake pans. Bake at 350 degrees for 30-35 minutes, or until a toothpick inserted near the center comes out clean. Cool for 10 minutes before removing from pans to wire racks to cool completely.

For frosting, in a small mixing bowl, beat the melted chips, cream cheese, vanilla and salt until light and fluffy. Add confectioner's sugar alternately with enough milk to achieve spreading consistency. Spread frosting between layers and over top and sides of cake. You may also use chocolate frosting for variation. Serves 12-14.

PECAN DELIGHTS (Cookies)

1/2 pound butter
4 Tablespoons granulated sugar
2 cups ground pecan nuts
2 cups all purpose flour

Combine all ingredients together and mix well. With clean hands, form into small balls. Bake at 250 degrees for 1 hour. Roll in powdered sugar while hot. Let cool, then roll in powdered sugar once more when cool. Keep in refrigerator.

PECAN PIE

2 cups all-purpose flour
2 Tablespoons granulated sugar
1 teaspoon plus a pinch of salt
1/2 pound butter, softened
5 egg yolks
2 Tablespoons cold water
1 cup brown sugar, packed
1 cup sorghum or heavy dark molasses
1 cup pecan meats, coarsely chopped
Pecan halves

Blend flour, sugar and 1 teaspoon salt. Cut in 1/4 pound butter until particles are size of small peas. Combine 1 egg yolk and cold water. Sprinkle over flour mixture, a Tablespoon at a time, mixing in with fork. Form dough into a ball and refrigerate 1/2 hour. Roll out and line 9" pie pan with dough; pierce dough several times with fork.

Blend brown sugar, pinch of salt and sorghum. Beat 4 egg yolks and add to sugar mixture. Add remaining 1/4 pound butter and chopped pecan meats. Blend well, then pour mixture into pie shell. Top with pecan halves arranged in circles from outer edge to center of pie. Bake at 400 degrees for 10 minutes, then turn oven down to 300 degrees and bake for another 35 minutes. Cool on rack before serving.

POMANDERS
(Cookies)

1 - 6 oz. Package chocolate chips
1/2 cup granulated sugar
1/4 cup corn syrup
1/4 cup water
2 1/2 cups finely crushed vanilla wafers
1 cup finely chopped nuts
1 teaspoon orange extract
Granulated sugar (tinted red and/or green for Christmas; pink, yellow and blue for Easter; red, white and blue for summer, etc.)

Melt chocolate chips over hot water in double boiler. Stir in granulated sugar and corn syrup. Blend in water. Combine wafers and nuts; add chocolate mix and orange extract. Mix well. Form into 1" balls. Roll balls in colored sugar. Let ripen in covered container several days. These wonderful cookies improve with age and also freeze well.

RUM BALLS (Cookies)

30 vanilla wafers, crushed
2 Tablespoons cocoa
2 Tablespoons Karo® corn syrup
1 cup finely chopped nuts
1/4 cup rum or whiskey

Mix all ingredients well in large bowl. With clean hands, form mixture into small balls. Roll balls in powdered sugar and store in an airtight container in the refrigerator. These cookies improve with age and keep at least 1 month.

SPELL-BINDERS (Cookies)

1 1/2 cups all purpose flour
1 1/2 teaspoons baking powder
1 teaspoon baking soda
1 cup brown sugar, firmly packed
1 cup softened butter or margarine
1 egg
1 cup quick cooking rolled oats
1 cup flaked coconut
1/2 cup + 2 Tablespoons finely crushed cornflakes
1 cup salted Spanish peanuts

Cream the butter and sugar together well, until light and fluffy. Sift the flour together with the baking powder and baking soda, and add to butter mixture gradually. Stir in rolled oats, 1/2 cup cornflake crumbs, coconut and peanuts. Drop by rounded teaspoon onto ungreased baking sheets. Flatten with the bottom of a drinking glass dipped in cornflake crumbs. Bake at 350 degrees for 12 - 15 minutes. Drizzle with icing (see below). Makes 4 dozen cookies.

Icing: Combine 4 Tablespoons melted butter, 2 cups powdered sugar, 2 Tablespoons hot water, 2 teaspoons vanilla. Beat to the consistency of a glaze.

TWO-TONE MALLOW BITES (Cookies)

2 - 6 oz. Packages (2 cups) butterscotch morsels
2 Tablespoons shortening (butter or Crisco®)
1 cup chopped walnuts'
2 cups miniature marshmallows
2 - 6 oz. Packages (or 1 - 12 oz. Package; 2 cups) semi-sweet chocolate morsels

Melt together over hot (not boiling) water, butterscotch morsels and 1 Tablespoon shortening. Stir in walnuts. Spread in a greased 9" square baking pan. Cover with even layer of marshmallows, gently pressing into surface. Melt together over hot (not boiling) water, semi-sweet chocolate morsels and remaining shortening. Spread evenly over marshmallow layer. If desired, garnish with additional chopped walnuts. Cool till firm, then cut into squares. Makes about 2 pounds.

Catty Notes

Menu Planners

"Cats are connoisseurs of comfort."
- James Herriott

DATE:
OCCASION:
 # OF GUESTS:
THEME:
SERVING STYLE (BUFFET OR SIT DOWN):

BEVERAGES:

APPETIZERS:

SOUPS/SALADS:

BREADS/CEREALS:

VEGETABLE DISH:

ENTREE:

DESSERT:

SHOPPING LIST:

NOTES:

Cooking Measurements & Conversions

"Who can believe that there is
no soul behind those luminous eyes!"
- Theophile Gautier

Basic U.S. Measurements

Pinch or dash (dry) = Less than 1/8 teaspoon
Dash (liquid) = A few drops
3 Teaspoons = 1 Tablespoon
1/2 Tablespoon = 1 1/2 Teaspoons
1 Tablespoon = 3 Teaspoons
2 Tablespoons = 1 fluid ounce
4 Tablespoons = 1/4 Cup
8 Tablespoons = 4 fluid ounces
12 Tablespoons = 2/3 Cup
16 Tablespoons = 1 Cup or 8 fluid ounces
48 Teaspoons = 1 Cup or 8 fluid ounces
1/8 Cup = 2 Tablespoons
1/4 Cup = 4 Tablespoons or 2 fluid ounces
1/3 Cup = 5 Tablespoons + 1 Teaspoon
1/2 Cup = 8 Tablespoons
1 Cup = 16 Tablespoons or 8 fluid ounces
1 Cup = 1/2 pint
2 Cups = 1 Pint
2 Pints = 1 Quart
4 Quarts (liquid) = 1 Gallon
8 Quarts (dry) = 1 Peck
4 Pecks (dry) = 1 Bushel

Metric to U.S. Measurements (Conversions)

1 Gram = .035 Ounce
30 Grams = 1 Ounce
55 Grams = 2 Ounces
225 Grams = 8 Ounces
455 Grams = 16 Ounces or 1 Pound
500 Grams = 1.1 Pounds
1 Kilogram = 2.2 Pounds
1 Milliliter = 1/5 Teaspoon
5 Milliliters = 1 Teaspoon
15 Milliliters = 1 Tablespoon
120 Milliliters = 1/2 Cup
240 Milliliters = 1 Cup
.95 Liter = 1 Quart
1 Liter = 1.06 Quart
3.8 Liters = 4 Quarts or 1 Gallon

Heat Temperatures in Fahrenheit and Centigrade
Degrees Fahrenheit and Degrees Centigrade

Boiling point of water 212° = 100°
Freezing point of water 32° = 0°

Fahrenheit = Celsius
200° = 95°
225° = 110°
250° = 120°
275° = 135°
300° = 150°
325° = 165°
350° = 175°
375° = 190°
400° = 200°
425° = 220°
450° = 230°
475° = 245°

"What greater gift than
the love of a cat?"
- Charles Dickens

Sandy Spots

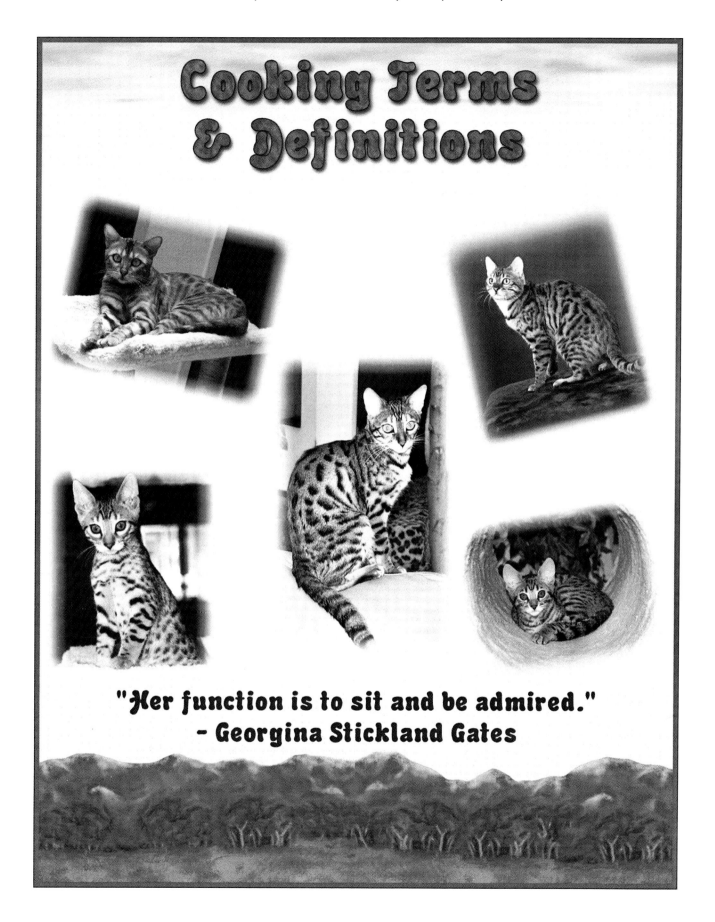

Cooking Terms & Definitions

"Her function is to sit and be admired."
- Georgina Stickland Gates

A

Aging: A term used to describe the holding of meats at a temperature of 34 to 36 degrees F. for a period of time to break down the tough connective tissues through the action of enzymes thus increasing tenderness.
Agneau: (French) Lamb.
a la: (French) The style of, such as: a la Francaise (The style of the French).
a la Bourgeoise: (French) The style of the family (family style).
a la Broche: (French) Cooked on a skewer over a flame. See Brochette.
a la Carte: (French) Each menu item is priced separately: Foods prepared to order.
a la King: (French) A Bechemel sauce containing mushrooms, green peppers, and red peppers or pimentos.
a la Mode: (French) Refers to ice cream on top of pie.
a la Provencale: (French) Dishes prepared with garlic and olive oil. See Provencale.
a la Russe: (French) The Russian way.
Allumette Potatoes: (French) Potatoes cut like large match sticks.
Amandine: (French) Prepared with or garnished with almonds.
Anglaise: (French) The English way.
A.P.: As Purchased.
Aspic: (English) Clear meat, poultry, or fish jelly.
au Gratin: (French) To top food with cheese or bread crumbs, then baked.
au Jus: (French) Served with natural juices.
au Lait: (French) With milk.
au Naturel: (French) Food that are plainly cooked.

B

Bake: To cook in an oven.
Bard: To wrap meat with bacon or salt pork.
Baste: To pour drippings, fat, or stock over food while cooking.
Batter: A mixture of flour and liquid.
Bean Sprouts: Chinese Mung beans.
Bearnaise: (French) Sauce derived from Hollandaise, with a tarragon reduction added.
Bechamel: (French) A rich cream sauce made from cream and a roux, with an onion pique.
Beef, Dried: Beef soaked in brine and then soaked and dried.
Beurre: (burr) (French) Butter.
Beurre Noir: (burr-nwahr) (French) Butter cooked to a dark brown, then adding capers and a dash of vinegar.
Beurre Noisette: (burr-nwah-zet) (French) Butter that tastes like hazelnuts, achieved by melting butter until it turns a golden brown.
Blanch: to partially cook vegetables by parboiling.

Braise: to brown meat, then cook slowly in a small amount of liquid. Used to tenderize tougher cuts of meat.

Buttercream frosting: the simplest kind of frosting, it is uncooked and made from confectioner's sugar, butter, milk and flavoring.

C

Cake pan: round baking pan with straight sides.

Cafe: (French) Coffee.

Calorie: Unit of heat; 1 calorie = 3.968 B.T.U. . The heat required to raise 1 gram of water 1 degree centigrade.

Canadian Bacon: Lean, trimmed, pressed, smoked pork loin.

Canape: (French) An appetizer prepared on a base such as toast or crackers.

Canard: (French) Duck.

Chaud: (French) Hot.

Chef: (French) A culinary expert. The chief of the kitchen.

Coddling: Cooking just below the boiling point; such as Coddled Eggs.

Cooked frosting: a more complicated, candy-like frosting, made from sugar, butter, flavoring and milk, and cooked on the stovetop.

Coquille: (French) Shell.

Cream (as in butter and sugar): a baking technique involving combining butter or margarine and sugar together to a fluffy consistency. Done by thoroughly beating butter in a bowl, then gradually adding sugar until mixture is fluffy and creamy.

Crepe: (French) Thin pancakes.

Cut in: using a pastry fork or pastry cutter, use cutting movements to mix dry ingredients with shortening, as in a pie crust. The end result should be small pea-sized bits.

D

De-glaze: to pour a small amount of liquid into a hot pan in which something has been fried, to clean the pan bottom, especially as for gravy.

Demi: (French) Half.

Diced: Cut into small cubes.

Double a recipe: to increase all recipe amounts times two. One cup of flour doubled is two cups and so on. Makes a recipe bigger.

Drawn butter: Melted butter.

Dredging: To coat with dry ingredients such as flour or bread crumbs.

Dusting: To sprinkle with sugar or flour.

E

Egg brush or wash: brushing the top of a baked item, such as bread, lightly with a beaten egg.

Emince (French) Cut fine, or sliced thin.

E.P.: Edible Portion.

Espagnole: A basic brown sauce.

F

Farci: Stuffed.
Farina: Inner portion of coarsely ground hard wheat.
Fold: to gently combine two ingredients, using a bottom-to-top motion with the spoon or scraper.
Forcemeat: Ground meat or meats, mixed with seasonings used for stuffing.
Froid: (French) Cold.

G

Garnish: To decorate. Also referring to the food used to decorate.
Garniture: French for garnish.
Gateau: (French) Cake.
Giblets: The trimmings from poultry such as the liver, heart, etc..
Gnocchi: Italian dumpling.
Gourmet: (French) Connoisseur of culinary delights.
Gravy: a thick sauce, usually made from pan drippings and other liquid, plus flour.

H

Halve a recipe: to cut the amounts of a recipe by 50 percent. One cup would become one-half cup, and so forth. Makes a recipe smaller.
Haricots Verts: Tiny green string beans.
Heifer: A young female cow that has not had a calf yet.
Herb Bouquet: A mixture of tied herbs used for seasoning in soups, sauces, and stocks.
Hors d'oeuvre: ("ohr-duh-vr") (French) Petite appetizers or relishes. Serve as the first course of the meal.

I

Infusion: Liquid derived from steeping herbs, spices, etc.
Insulated baking sheet: a cookie sheet or jellyroll pan that has a two-layer bottom.

J

Jellyroll pan: a baking pan, usually 9½" by 13", with sides about an inch high. Also good for use as a cookie sheet.
Julienne: to cut vegetables in finger-length, narrow strips, usually against the grain at an angle. Often used in stir-fry dishes.
Jus: Usually refers to the natural juice from meat. See au Jus.

K

Karo: Light or dark corn Syrup.
Kasha: Buckwheat grouts.
Kitchen Bouquet: A trade name a bottled sauce flavor and color enhancer.
Knead: another bread-making term, refers to the folding and working motion used to make the dough elastic in consistency.
Kosher: (meat) Meat sold within 48 hours after being butchered in accordance to Hebrew religious laws. The style of Jewish dietary cooking.
Kumquats: Small oval citrus fruit that is golden-orange in color.

L

Lait: (French) Milk.
Larding: Salt pork strips inserted into meat with a special needle. Used to add flavor and moisture to meat.
Lardons: Julienne of bacon. Strips of salt pork used for larding.
Leek: Small onion like plant, used as an aromatic seasoning or vegetable.
Legumes: (French) Dried beans, peas, lentils and such.
Lentil: A brown or yellow flat seed resembling a pea used for soups, garnishes, and as a vegetable.
Liaison: A binding agent made up of egg yolks and cream, used for thickening soups and sauces.
Lyonnaise Potatoes: (French) Potatoes sliced and sautéed with onions.

M

Mace: The outer shell of nutmeg (seasoning).
Manhattan Clam Chowder: Made with quahog clams, tomatoes, onions, celery, and potatoes.
Maraschino: An Italian cherry cordial. Also cherries.
Marsala: Semi-dry, pale golden, Italian wine from Sicily.
Menthe: (French) Mint.
Meringue: a baking term used to refer to the shells made from egg white and flavoring, and filled with a sweet filling, or to the egg whites on a pie, and browned in the oven.
Minced: Ground or chopped fine.

N

Navarin: (French) Lamb stew with root vegetables, cut green beans, tomatoes, and peas.
Noir: (French) Black.
Nouilles: (French) Noodles.

O

O'Brien: With diced pimiento and green pepper

Oeuf: (French) Egg.
Okra: A vegetable pod used mainly in gumbos, but also other soups, and served as a vegetable.
Oleo: a term for margarine often found in older cookbooks. A stick of oleo is a stick of margarine.
Omelet: Seasoned eggs that are beaten and fried. The eggs will puff up at which time, they are rolled or folded over.

P

Pan Broiling: To cook in an uncovered skillet where the fat is poured off during cooking.
Papaya: A sweet tropical fruit. The juice of this fruit yields an enzyme that is used as a meat tenderizer.
Papillote: (French) Cooked in foil or parchment paper to seal in flavor, then served and cut open at table.
Paprika: Used as a seasoning or coloring agent, this is the ground dried fruit of various ripe pepper plants.
Parboiling: To cook partially by boiling for a short period of time.
Peche: (French) Peach.
Petit: (French) Small.
Pie pan: round baking pan with slanted sides.
Pinch/dash: small, inexact amount you could pick up between your thumb and first finger that basically means seasoning per your own taste.
Punch down: a term used in working with yeast-risen products. After letting the dough rise, one flattens it forcefully in the bowl before turning it out onto a floured board.

Q

Quenelle: A poached dumpling (oval), usually made of veal or chicken.
Quiche: A pie made of custard and cheese.

R

Ragout: (French) Stew.
Raisin: Dried grape.
Ramekin: Small shallow baking dish. The foods cooked in these are also served in them.
Rasher: Thin slice of bacon or a portion consisting of 3 slices of bacon.
Rest: in bread-making, to let the dough sit a few minutes before kneading more.
Rise: in bread-making, to leave the dough in a warm place and allow to double in volume.
Rolling boil: when substance is boiling sufficiently that stirring with a spoon does not cause it to stop boiling.

Royal icing: a hard icing used for decorating purposes. This icing becomes solid quickly. It is often used on cookies. The icing, once hard, does not soften.

S

Sabayon: A sauce resembling custard, mainly used for puddings or vanilla ice cream. Sabayon is made of wine, sugar, and egg yolks.

Saccharin: A product made from coal tar, used as a substitute for sugar. Saccharin has no food value.

Sachet bag: Cloth bag filled with select herbs used to season soups or stocks.

Saffron: The pistil of the Crocus plant, used for flavoring or coloring of food.

Sauce: food topping (may or may not be cooked) made from any ingredients on hand, including butter, flour and milk, or even eggs.

Saute: to quickly brown vegetables or meat in a small amount of fat.

Scald (as in milk): to heat milk just to the point that steam is rising from it, but not to boiling.

Scraper/spatula: these terms are sometimes used interchangeably. Technically, a spatula is used to turn food in a pan, such as pancakes. A scraper is a flat, flexible piece of rubber attached to a handle. These are useful for scraping food down the sides of a pan or bowl.

Sear: to quickly brown the outside of meat at a high temperature.

Simple syrup: a syrup that results from cooking water and sugar together until boiling.

Soft ball/soft crack; hard ball/hard crack: these are candy-making terms that denote what a ball of the candy does when placed in a cup of cold water. A good candy thermometer will have these stages noted on it.

Springform pan: a round cake pan with straight sides that come away from the cake separately. Often used for cheesecakes.

T

Tabasco: Hot red pepper sauce (brand name).

Toss: To mix with a rising and falling action.

Tripe: The edible lining of stomach (beef).

Truss: To bind poultry for roasting with string or skewers.

Tube pan: a round cake pan with tall, smooth sides and a metal tube in the middle. Often used for angel food cake, but an excellent all-purpose cake pan. A Bundt pan is a type of tube pan, with fluted sides.

U

Unsaturated fat: A kind of fat that is in liquid form at room temperature.

V

Vert: (French) Green.
Viande: (French) Meat.

W

Waldorf Salad: A salad made with apples, celery, nuts, whip cream, and mayonnaise on a bed of lettuce.

X

Y

Yams: Sweet potato.
Yorkshire pudding: A batter made with flour, eggs, salt, and milk that is baked with standing rib roast (prime rib).

Z

Zest: Citrus rind.
Zucchini: Green Italian squash.

Catty Cookbook Index

"Cats are absolute individuals, with their own ideas about everything, including the people they own."
- John Dingman

G

Galliano, 2
Garlic, 10, 12, 13, 14, 15, 18, 19, 21, 22, 26, 27, 28, 29, 30, 32, 45, 46, 47, 48, 52, 56, 58, 59, 60, 61, 62, 80
Gazpacho, 28
German Chocolate, 65
Gingerbread, 38
Gold Fingers, 13
Golden Cadillac, 2
Gouda, 11
Graham Cracker, 64, 65, 69
Grape, 69, 84
Grapefruit, 3, 6, 7, 21
Grasshopper Pie, 67
Green Beans, 27, 46, 83
Grilled, 46, 56
Ground Beef, 15, 29, 52, 53, 61, 62
Gruyere, 15, 20, 56
Guacamole, 13, 60

H

Halibut, 57
Ham, 10, 11, 12, 26, 40, 56, 57, 62
Honey, 27, 48, 57, 69
Honeydew, 19, 27

I

Instant Coffee, 2, 3, 65, 66

J

Jack Cheese, 10, 13, 47
Jalapeno, 12, 14, 37
Jello, 18, 21, 22
Juice, 2, 3, 4, 6, 7, 8, 12, 13, 14, 18, 19, 21, 22, 23, 26, 27, 28, 30, 35, 38, 39, 44, 47, 52, 54, 55, 56, 57, 58, 59, 60, 62, 64, 68, 69, 82, 84

K

Kahlua, 2, 3, 67
Karo, 34, 71, 83
Ketchup, 45

L

Lard, 38, 60
Lasagna, 52, 53, 54
Lemon, 2, 3, 4, 6, 7, 8, 12, 13, 14, 18, 19, 21, 22, 23, 26, 27, 28, 38, 44, 47, 52, 54, 55, 56, 58, 59, 60, 64, 68
Lemon Bars, 68
Lemonade, 6, 7
Lettuce, 18, 19, 20, 21, 22, 23, 26, 86
Lima Bean, 26
Limeade, 3
Liqueur, 2
Liver, 59, 82
Lobster, 21
London Broil, 57

M

Mallow Bites, Two-Tone, 71
Mango, 57
Maple, 40
Margarine, 10, 11, 27, 34, 37, 39, 45, 47, 49, 59, 62, 64, 66, 67, 68, 69, 71, 81, 84
Margarita, 3, 68
Marinade, 47, 52, 53, 56
Marjoram, 15, 55, 60
Marshmallow, 67, 71
Mayonnaise, 12, 15, 18, 19, 20, 21, 23, 36, 44, 55, 59, 86
Measurements & Conversions, 75
Meat, 21, 30, 52, 53, 54, 55, 57, 61, 62, 80, 81, 82, 83, 84, 85, 86
Meatball, 15, 29
Melon, 8, 19, 22, 27
Metric, 76
Mini-Quiche, 10
Mint, 7, 8, 14, 19, 22, 27, 28, 65, 69, 83
Mocha, 66

Scalloped, 44
Scallops, 52
Scampi, 60
Scones, 36, 37
Scotch, 30
Shallot, 56
Sherry, 11, 26, 48, 52, 60
Shrimp, 10, 18, 21, 27, 54, 60
Singapore Sling, 4
Smoothie, 6
Snuggler, 4
Soda, 4, 6, 7, 29, 34, 38, 39, 41, 49
Sole, 58
Soufflé, 44, 67
Soup, 26, 27, 28, 29, 30, 31, 32, 48, 54, 55, 59, 60
Sour Cream, 10, 11, 12, 18, 19, 20, 26, 30, 31, 35, 37, 38, 40, 44, 45, 46, 48, 53, 60, 61, 66
Sourdough, 29, 36, 52
Soy, 18, 34, 47, 55, 59
Spaghetti, 49, 61
Spell-Binders (cookies), 71
Spiced, 3
Spinach, 15, 20, 31, 32, 45
Split Pea, 27
Squash, 22, 86
Steak, 52, 57
Stew, 28, 83, 84
Strawberry, 7, 40
Sugar, 2, 3, 6, 7, 8, 18, 21, 22, 27, 34, 35, 36, 37, 38, 39, 40, 41, 44, 46, 48, 49, 50, 64, 65, 66, 67, 68, 69, 70, 71, 81, 85
Summer, 22, 26, 27, 70
Sun Tea, 8
Swedish, 34
Sweet and Sour, 15, 22
Sweet Onion, 21
Swiss, 10, 21, 36, 45, 46, 49, 56, 62

T

Tabasco, 11, 12, 30, 31, 46, 60, 85
Tarragon, 26, 27, 28, 57, 80
Tea, 8

Teriyaki, 46
Thyme, 19, 26, 29, 30, 45, 46, 53, 54, 55, 60
Tomato, 13, 14, 15, 20, 21, 22, 27, 28, 29, 30, 31, 32, 40, 48, 49, 50, 52, 53, 54, 55, 57, 59, 60, 62, 83
Torte, 65
Tortilla, 13, 14, 30, 53, 60
Triple Sec, 2, 3, 69
Tuna, 20

V

Vanilla, 2, 3, 6, 7, 35, 38, 40, 64, 65, 66, 67, 68, 69, 70, 71, 85
Veal, 32, 84
Vegetable, 19, 27, 30, 40, 44, 45, 47, 74, 83, 84
Velveeta®, 12
Vinegar, 18, 20, 21, 22, 28, 57, 69, 80

W

Wafer, 64, 65, 66
Walnut, 12
Watermelonade, 8
Wedding Bell Soup, 32
Wheat, 34, 36, 82
Whipped Cream, 2, 4, 6, 18, 64, 65, 66, 67, 69
Whiskey, 1, 71
White Rice, 29, 45, 55, 58
Wild Rice, 55, 62
Wine, 3, 18, 20, 21, 22, 27, 28, 31, 48, 52, 56, 59, 83, 85
Worcestershire, 11, 12, 13, 28, 30, 57, 59, 61

Y

Yam, 48
Yeast, 34, 36, 37, 40, 84
Yogurt, 19, 20, 61, 69

Z

Zucchini, 22, 27, 29, 30, 41, 49, 50, 53, 61, 62, 86

Coming Soon

from Holly D. Webber (with Sunny Spots) & Cedar Hill Publishing

Two NEW
CATTY
COOKBOOKS

Especially for
COOKIE LOVERS

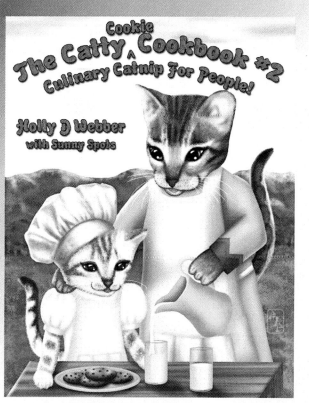

Where can I get more books?

Do you like this cookbook? Would you like to order some for your cat-loving friends?

Ordering Information

Copies of "The Catty Cookbook" are $29.95 each, plus $5.00 shipping/handling.
Three or more are $24.95 each, plus $3.00 shipping/handling per copy.
Purr-sonally autographed copies available for an additional $5.00.

Order directly from the authors online at **www.cattycookbook.com** or fill out and mail/fax the order form below.

Billing Information:

Name _____

Address _____

City, State, Zip _____

Daytime Phone _____

Shipping Information: (if different)

Name _____

Address _____

City, State, Zip _____

Daytime Phone _____

No. of books ordered: _____ x $ _____ = $ _____

Autographed? (how many) _____ x $ 5.00 = $ _____

Shipping/Handling _____ x $ _____ = $ _____

ORDER TOTAL: $ _____

Payment Options: VISA, Mastercard, money orders or cashier checks payable to "Foothill Felines".

Card Number: _____ Exp. Date: _____

Mail or fax your order form to: Foothill Felines, P.O. Box 418104, Sacramento CA 95841-8104. Fax: (916) 481-CATS.

Thank you!